.Popular and imp
simplified and mo
old t

Stories from Herodotus

STORIES
FROM HERODOTUS

A PANORAMA OF EVENTS AND PEOPLES
OF THE ANCIENT WORLD

Selected and Translated by
Glanville Downey

Illustrated by Enrico Arno

E. P. Dutton & Co., Inc.   New York

For L. V. A.

Foreword

WHY IT IS IMPORTANT
TO READ HERODOTUS TODAY

FOR MORE THAN two thousand years, students of what we now call "high school age" have found the reading of Herodotus fascinating and rewarding. His writings have weathered the passing of the years, with the vast changes they have wrought, and are still read by students on every continent of the globe. Why is it that Herodotus is read today with profit and with pleasure? The answer is that the manner of his writing absorbs the attention of the reader, and the matter is as timeless as man's interest in his fellow man and in the ever-recurring struggle for human liberty.

When Herodotus writes of his travels, he conveys to us a tremendous amount of illuminating information about the places to which he went, the people he saw, their customs, their way of life, their history, their sorrows, and their glories. It is to Herodotus that we are indebted for some of the basic facts about ancient history and, in addition, for many charming anecdotes and gossipy accounts of the great men of antiquity.

We can picture Herodotus now, as he went about his travels, the father, not only of historians, but also of tourists. Having no camera, the ever-present companion of the modern tourist, Herodotus had to rely on his powers of observation, his constant questioning of natives, and his ability to describe in vivid language what he had observed and learned. How fortunate the world is that his eyes were so keen, his questions so searching, and his literary style so fascinating! These qualities have made his writings live as a precious heritage of knowledge about ancient people and places.

The question of the reliability of Herodotus' account has always provided a challenge to his more thoughtful readers. In many instances, he is merely repeating the information (or misinformation) given to him by persons with whom he spoke during his travels. In others, he tells us what he himself saw. For centuries, many readers doubted the truth of some of Herodotus' statements, but modern archaeological findings are beginning to corroborate the truth of much that he reported.

Interesting and valuable as the record of his travels is for modern readers, the account of the Persian Wars is even more exciting. Herodotus not only vividly tells the story of the war between the Greeks and the Persian empire, but, in order to show how glorious the

Greek victory was, writes a history of the mighty Persian empire which is the principal source of our knowledge of that subject. Just as we are indebted to the Roman historian Livy for much of our knowledge about Hannibal, the great enemy of Rome, so we must read Herodotus if we are to understand the Persian enemies of Greece.

It is important for thinking men to know the course of events that produced their civilization. Herodotus realized this. He said that his purpose in writing was to ensure that the deeds of the men of his day would not be obliterated by time. He felt that the struggle which the Greeks had waged for freedom from Persian tyranny was one of the decisive events in the development of civilization and therefore deserved to be remembered by future ages.

The struggle for human liberty never ends. It is still with us. In our efforts to promote liberty, we can derive courage and strength from Herodotus' account of the heroic struggle of the Greeks to preserve their liberty when it was threatened by Persian despotism.

SYLVIA W. GERBER
Teacher of Latin
Woodrow Wilson High School
Washington, D. C.

Contents

Introduction

HERODOTUS AND HIS BOOK

"THE FATHER OF HISTORY"—the first writer of history as we know it in Europe and America—had to be a person of unusual gifts. Herodotus was such a person. His gifts were so remarkable, in fact, that he is not only the first of our historians, but one of the greatest.

Herodotus was born at about the time of the Persian Wars—that is, about 480 B.C.—in Halicarnassus, one of the Greek cities on the western coast of Asia Minor. He was a member of one of the prominent families in the city and had a good education. In common with many other independent Greek cities at that time, Halicarnassus suffered from internal struggles for the political control of the city; and when one of Herodotus' relatives, a prominent citizen, was killed by a political "strong man" who was trying to make himself sole master of Halicarnassus, Herodotus left the city and went to Samos to live. It was soon after this that he began his travels. When he had finished his travels and had begun to work on his book, he lived in Athens for a time, and then joined the colony which Athens established at Thurii, in southern Italy, in 443 B.C. It is evident from the pages of his book that Herodotus liked and admired the Athenians, and they in turn respected him. When he died at Thurii, the city set up an honorific statue of him, and this and his tomb were shown to visitors. For a long time he was commonly known as "Herodotus of Thurii," until Halicarnassus at length claimed him, setting up a statue to him and showing his portrait on the city's coins.

Herodotus had the financial means, and the curiosity, to travel widely, in a day when travel was slow and not always comfortable or safe. There is a famous passage in his book (translated on one of the last pages in this volume) in which Herodotus describes the devotion to duty of the hardy mounted couriers of the Persian king who carried messages along the Royal Highway between Sardis and Susa. "Neither snow nor rain nor heat nor darkness keep them from completing their appointed course," Herodotus writes; and we may be sure that he himself had encountered snow, rain, heat, and darkness in his own journeys. His book shows that he had visited Egypt extensively, had gone all the way to Babylon and perhaps on to Susa (Susa was twelve hundred miles from the Greek coast of Asia Minor), had visited the Black Sea and the steppes of the Ukraine, had taken part in the founding of a Greek colony in southern Italy, and had made excursions to some of the Greek cities on the coast of northern Africa. No other Greek, so far as we know, had ever traveled so widely.

In those days, with few books and no newspapers, travel was the only way to see the world and learn about its people and its lands. Herodotus loved people and was continually interested in them. He was curious about everything; the title of his book in Greek, *Historiai,* means *Inquiries.*

This interest in people and his friendly curiosity were matched by another special gift. Herodotus was a born storyteller and a born writer. As a writer he had perfect taste, first in choosing what to write about, and then in choosing the simplest and most effective way to describe it. The simplicity and clarity of his writing are deceptive; actually they conceal great art and great skill, as everyone who has ever written anything will recognize. Behind the style, we can see an attractive human being.

Herodotus had two themes. First, he wished to in-

GREECE and PERSIA
at the time of the Persian War

- - -> Xerxes' army
· · · ·> the Persian fleet

Chersonese
Hellespont
Abydos

MYSIA

Clazomenæ   Sardis
ONIA   LYDIA
Samos   Ephesus

Miletus
Branchidæ

Halicarnassus

EUXINE SEA

Sinope   PONTUS
Halys R.
CAPPADOCIA
Sardis
LYDIA   Calynda   CILICIA

Cyprus

ANEAN SEA   Sidon
Tyre
PHOENICIA

EGYPT   Nile R.

CASPIAN SEA

Mardi

P   E   R   S   I   A
MEDIA
MESOPOTAMIA
Tigris R.   ASSIA
Euphrates R.   Susa

Babylon   PERSIAN GULF   Persepolis

ARABIA

form his fellow Greeks about the whole known world of their time. Most of the Greeks who read his book, or heard it read aloud, were ignorant of practically everything concerning the countries he visited; and it was because he had an original mind and a love of the human race that Herodotus made it his life work to collect his information and write the kind of book he planned. No one before him had had such a vision of what a book might be.

It was literally up to Herodotus to discover what the world was like, who the people were who lived in it, and how they lived. No one before him had conducted the sort of historical research he undertook. He had a few written sources concerning special areas of geography and history, but these were not complete, and it was obvious that they were not always trustworthy. Herodotus determined to see things for himself. When he went to Egypt he found an enormous number of things that would be interesting and unusual to his Greek friends. He learned all he could about Egyptian daily life that made it different from Greek life; he described carefully such varied things as the anatomy and habits of the crocodile, methods of embalming, the way in which the Egyptians did their marketing, and the periodic flooding of the Nile. He measured the size of the pyramids by pacing along the sides—and his measurements are remarkably correct.

Herodotus was sometimes deceived by his local interpreters and his guides, and he had a weakness for large numbers—witness the fantastic computation of the size of the Persian army—but we never find him consciously telling a lie. He describes the great city of Babylon—one of the extraordinary sights of the ancient world—with great care, and some of the details of his description—the method of constructing the walls, the tower of the sanctuary of Bel, the characteristics of Persian education and religion—have been confirmed by modern archaeological discoveries and historical research. Herodotus allows us to see the surprise and even admiration he felt for some of the things he learned in Persia.

Herodotus' journey to the Black Sea and the Russian steppes was a real adventure. Somehow—perhaps with a convoy of traders—he seems to have gotten up the Dnieper River to a region near Kiev, where he saw the tombs of the Scythian kings. His account of these tombs, and of the customs of the Scythians, which to a Greek would seem bizarre, we now know are quite accurate. He mentions a strange tree and its fruit, unknown in Europe; and we know that what he says is not an invention, for he describes the cherry tree, which was only brought to Western countries later.

The innumerable details that Herodotus sets down are of absorbing interest to the modern reader, as they were to Herodotus' own audience. But Herodotus had another theme, the conflict of Greece and Persia. For

Herodotus and his generation, this was the decisive epoch in the history of Greece, the ordeal in which the independence of Greece was established. But for Herodotus it was even more than a prolonged military struggle. It was the epic conflict of two different types of civilization, two contrasting ways of life, represented by the enslaved Persian and the free Greek. The contrast between the Orient and Greece is well brought out in the story of the proud and self-satisfied eastern potentate Croesus and the thoughtful, detached Greek, Solon. It is typical of Herodotus' purpose that he tells the story in order to illustrate a lesson concerning human conduct and human fate. Croesus had been a spectacular figure in the century before Herodotus lived, and his reign (ca. 560-546 B.C.) made him an excellent subject for a tale with a moral lesson. In a world in which kings were expected to be wealthy, the last king of Lydia was so fantastically wealthy that to be "rich as Croesus" has remained a proverbial saying to this day.

For his story of the wars, Herodotus has been called "the Homer of the Persian Wars," and, like Homer, he took pains to show the motivations of human nature and human conduct that were involved. The story of Greece and Persia, as Herodotus has preserved it, was so decisive for the history of civilization that it is this part of his book which has been chosen for translation here. We are thrilled by the epic struggle between the autocratic kings of Persia and the democratic—if often quarrelsome—Greeks. The odds against the Greeks seem overwhelming, but it is Greek character and Greek bravery that win, and we can feel the pleasure Herodotus had in depicting the love of independence which, as he said, distinguished the Greeks from all other peoples. This part of Herodotus' book is one of the immortal chapters in the history of Western civilization, and it shows us one of the essential bases of our own historical and cultural heritage.

Herodotus' book has rightly been called a study in the history of civilization. He was the first to see the possibilities of history written on a grand scale. At the same time, Herodotus always wrote in human terms. An ancient literary critic wrote that "if we pick up his book, we admire it to the last syllable, and always want more."

And now a note about the translation. I have translated from the Greek, using the edition of Herodotus in the Loeb Classical Library by A. D. Godley, in four volumes (London, Heinemann; Cambridge, Harvard University Press). I have gratefully consulted the translation in that edition as well as the excellent version by A. de Selincourt in the Penguin Classics. For English readers, what is still the best edition is the famous translation of George Rawlinson, with notes, first issued in 1858, which has become almost an English classic itself. This has been so steadily in demand that an edition first published in the Everyman's Library (volumes 405, 406) in 1910 has been regularly reprinted, the last time in 1964.

At times I have simplified and condensed Herodotus' sentences, or omitted details that would be of little interest for the readers of the present book. In a few cases, when I have had to omit a considerable passage, I have supplied a few sentences by way of a bridge. When necessary, I have added a few words to explain ancient weights, measures, money and so on. But most of what is here is what Herodotus himself wrote. I hope that those who read this book will go on some time to enjoy Herodotus as he should be enjoyed—at leisure and on a large scale.

It is a great pleasure to thank my friend Mrs. Gerber for supplying the Foreword. Mrs. Gerber can speak with authority, for she is one of the most respected and successful teachers of the history and literature of the ancient world, and what she has written here represents a long experience in introducing young people to the classical writers.

GLANVILLE DOWNEY

Croesus, King of Lydia

CROESUS AND THE GREEKS

KING CROESUS RULED not only his own land, Lydia, but all the peoples who lived in the western part of Asia Minor. He was the first foreign ruler to have dealings with Greeks. Along the western Asia Minor coast, he conquered various groups of Greeks, called the Ionians, the Aeolians, and the Dorians, according to the dialects of Greek they spoke. These were the people that Croesus conquered. But his ambition did not stop there, and in order to extend his influence, he made a treaty of friendship with the Spartans who lived in mainland Greece.

Croesus was thirty-five years old when his father died and he came to the throne in his capital city, Sardis. He determined to conquer the Greek cities to the west of Lydia, and first of all besieged Ephesus. This was on the pretext that the Greeks had injured him, but actually of course he wished to extend his power. In this way, sometimes having to invent excuses, he declared war on all the Ionian and Aeolian cities, making a separate accusation in each case.

When Croesus had subdued all the Greeks along the coast and forced them to pay tribute to him, he began to make plans to build ships and attack the Greeks who lived on the islands in the Aegean Sea.

At this point a certain Greek traveler visited Sardis, a man of such distinction that Croesus invited him to the palace and asked him for news of what was happening among the Greeks.

"O King," the visitor replied, "the people of the islands are buying ten thousand horses and are going to attack Sardis."

Croesus was delighted. The islanders were seafaring people and knew nothing about managing horses. "May the gods really put it in their minds," the King said, "to come against my people on horseback!" This would mean sure defeat for the Greeks, fighting in a way they were not used to.

The visitor saw what the king was thinking. He answered, "O King, you are right when you hope to catch the island people riding horses on the mainland. But do you not realize that the islanders are praying that they may catch the people of Lydia in ships?"

Croesus saw the point. The Lydians were an inland people, as unused to sailing as the island Greeks were unused to riding. So he changed his plans, and decided to try to make friends with the Greeks of the islands.

CROESUS AND SOLON

As Croesus expanded his power, Sardis became a wealthy city, and all the leading teachers of Greece came to see it when they traveled to see the world. One of these was the famous Athenian Solon, who had drawn up a new constitution and code of laws for his native city. When the laws had been adopted, Solon left Athens to spend ten years traveling, to study the customs of the rest of the world and to give the people of Athens a chance to put his laws into effect without what they might think was interference from himself. He first went to Egypt, then visited Sardis, and the king was glad to entertain such a celebrated visitor in the palace.

When Solon had been a guest in the palace for three or four days, Croesus ordered his servants to take Solon around the royal treasuries to see all his abundant riches. When Solon had seen everything and had examined the treasures as thoroughly as he could, Croesus said, "Well, my Athenian friend, great reports have come to us concerning your wisdom and your travels, and how you have made long journeys to see the world, seeking knowledge. I have an urgent desire to ask you a question: whether you have ever seen a man who is more fortunate than anyone else in the world."

Croesus asked this question because he thought that he himself was the most fortunate man in the world. But Solon refused to flatter him, and said what he thought was the truth. "O King, I have seen such a man, an Athenian named Tellus."

Croesus was surprised, and said, rather sharply, "How do you judge that Tellus was the most fortunate in the world?"

Solon replied, "Tellus' city was prosperous and he had noble sons, and he lived long enough to see children born to all of them, and to see that they were able to keep their property. And then, when his life had been a good one, as we judge it, a most glorious end to this life was given to him. In a battle between the Athenians and the people of the neighboring city of

Eleusis, he fought for his city and routed the enemy, and died the noble death of a soldier; and the people of Athens gave him the great honor of a public funeral on the spot where he fell."

Solon told the story of Tellus and his many blessings as a kind of lesson for Croesus; but the king, thinking that he himself would deserve at least the second place, asked who, among the people Solon had seen, was the most fortunate after Tellus.

Solon answered, "Two men from Argos named Cleobis and Biton. They had enough property to live on; and in addition to this they had strength of body, which I will tell you about. They were both prize-winning athletes; but this is the story that was told about them. When the people of Argos were celebrating the annual festival of the goddess Hera, the custom of the festival required that the mother of these two young men must be driven to the temple of the goddess in an oxcart. But the oxen did not come in from the fields in time. So the two young men, when they saw there was no time to lose, put themselves into harness and dragged the heavy oxcart along, with their mother sitting in it. They drew it for nearly six miles, and came to the temple. Everyone at the festival saw them arrive.

"Then they had the finest kind of death, a proof from heaven that such a death can be noble. The men of Argos crowded round and congratulated the young men on their strength, and the women told the mother how fortunate she was to possess such sons. And the mother, rejoicing in what had been done and in what had been said about it, went to the temple of Hera and stood before the statue of the goddess; and she prayed that the goddess would give to her sons Cleobis and Biton, who had honored her so greatly, the finest gift a human being can receive.

"After this prayer, all the people performed the usual sacrifices to the goddess and held the customary feast. Since their mother had just prayed to the goddess for them, the two young men went to sleep in the temple. But they never woke up, and that was the end of their lives. The people of Argos had statues of them made and had them set up in Delphi, because of the excellence of their lives."

Croesus was irritated with Solon for giving the second prize for good fortune to these two young men. He spoke angrily, "You guest from Athens! What of my prosperity? Is it so worthless that you do not even compare me with ordinary men?"

"Croesus," Solon answered, "what you are asking me about is the fate of human beings. I know that heaven is jealous of human affairs and loves to trouble us. As time goes on, there is much to see that a man does not wish to see, and much to suffer. I put the limit of a man's life at seventy years. In these seventy years there are 25,555 days. Not one of these days is like another in what it brings. If this is so, Croesus, you can see that man's life is a thing of chance. If I am to speak of you, you seem to me to be very rich and the king of many men. But as for your question, I cannot answer you before I hear that you have ended your life well. The man who is very rich is not better than the man who has just enough for the day, unless good luck allows him to end his life with all his affairs in good order. Many very rich men are unhappy, and many men of average means are to be considered fortunate. The rich man has two advantages over the poor man: it is easier for him to carry out his wishes, and bad luck means less to him when it comes. The poor man is not exposed to the same kind of misfortune that comes to the rich man on account of his riches. The good fortune of the poor man is to be free from physical defects, illness, and any other kind of evil; and, though he is poor, he can find happiness in his children and his good health.

"If, in addition to this, such a man comes to a good ending of his life, that man is the one you are seeking— the man that has enjoyed every good thing that can possibly come to him, and is worthy to be called blessed. But until he dies, we must wait, and call him, not yet wholly blessed, but only fortunate. It is impossible for a man—since he is only a human being— to enjoy all these good things at the same time, just as no country produces everything that it needs and so is self-sufficient. It has one thing, but lacks another. The best land, of course, is the one that has most.

"Just so, no one human being is sufficient for himself. He may have one thing, but he lacks something else. It is the man who possesses most things while he is alive, and in the end has an honorable death, who in my opinion, O King, is worthy to bear the name of blessed. We must examine the end of every matter, to see how it turns out. Heaven gives many people a glimpse of blessedness, and then ruins them completely."

Solon got no reward from Croesus for saying this. The king sent him away and put no value on him, for he thought he was very stupid if he disregarded existing prosperity, such as Croesus had, and instead told him to watch for the end of every affair. But after Solon left, the righteous anger of heaven fell heavily on Croesus; and it seems to me that this was because he thought he himself was more worthy to be called blessed than all other men.

CROESUS AND
THE ORACLES

There was an ancient quarrel between the royal houses
of Lydia and Persia, going back five generations before
the time of Croesus. Having this cause for a quarrel
with Cyrus, the king of Persia, Croesus desired to make
war on the Persians, in order to avenge the injury done
to his ancestors, and in order to forestall the power
of the Persians, which was growing.

Having formed this plan in his mind, he determined
to try the oracles, both those in Greece and those in
Libya, and he sent messengers separately to the various
places—to Delphi, to Abae in Phocis, and to Dodona,
while others were sent to the oracular shrines of the
legendary heroes Amphiaraus and Trophonius. Others
were sent to Branchidae in the territory of the city of
Miletus.

These were the Greek oracles to which Croesus sent
for responses to his questions; and he ordered others

of his servants to go to inquire of the oracle of Ammon in Libya. He sent to the oracles this time in order to test them to find out how much they knew, so that if he found that they knew the truth, he might send a second time and ask whether he should undertake a campaign against the Persians.

When he sent to test these oracles, he gave the following orders to his servants: They were to keep count of the time after they left Sardis, and on the hundredth day after their departure they were to ask of the oracles what Croesus was doing on that day. They were to write down whatever the oracles said and bring the answers back to him.

What the other oracles said has not been preserved; but at Delphi, as soon as the Lydians came into the hall to address the god and put the question that had been laid upon them, the priestess of Apollo spoke in hexameter verses, as follows:

> I can count grains of sand and measure the contents of
> the ocean;
> I can understand what dumb men say, and I can hear
> when a man is not speaking;
> But now I smell a tortoise, with its strong shell
> Cooked in a bronze vessel, with the flesh of a lamb.
> Bronze is beneath it, and bronze is above it.

The Lydians wrote down these inspired words of the

Pythian priestess and went away and returned to Sardis. And when the others who had been sent around to various places came back bringing their oracles, Croesus unfolded them and glanced over each of the writings. Some of them were not at all satisfactory. But when he learned what had come from Delphi, he welcomed it with praise and thanksgiving. He considered that Delphi possessed the only true oracle, because it had found out what he himself was doing at the time. For after he had sent his messengers to the oracles, he thought of a device which it would be impossible to guess. He waited until the day that had been arranged and, with his own hands, cut up a tortoise and a lamb and boiled them in a bronze vessel with a bronze lid.

This then was the answer that came from Delphi to Croesus. As for the answer that came from the oracle of Amphiaraus, I cannot say what the oracle replied to the Lydians when they had done everything that was proper at the temple. Nothing of this oracle is recorded, except that Croesus considered that here, too, he had received a true answer.

After this he set out to win the favor of the god in Delphi with great sacrifices. Of the different kinds of animals that were customarily used in sacrifices, he slaughtered three thousand of each. He made a great pile and burned couches covered with gold and silver, golden cups, and purple cloaks and tunics. He did this in the hope of winning the god to his interests. He also commanded all the people of Lydia to sacrifice to the god whatever each one of them could.

When this part of the sacrifice was completed, Croesus melted down a vast quantity of gold and made it into bricklike shapes. The longer side was the length of six palms of the hand, and the height was one palm. There were a hundred and seventeen of these. Four of them were of refined gold, each one weighing two and a half talents or about a hundred and forty pounds. The others were of gold with alloy, and they weighed two talents or about a hundred and sixteen pounds each. He also ordered a statue of a lion to be made, of refined gold, weighing ten talents or almost five hundred and eighty pounds. When the temple in Delphi was burned, the lion fell from the gold bars which served as its base. It now lies in the treasury of the Corinthians, but it weighs only six and a half talents, for three and a half talents were melted away in the fire.

When these offerings were ready, Croesus sent them off to Delphi along with other gifts: two very large bowls, one gold and one silver. The gold one stood to the right as one entered the temple, the silver one to the left. These were removed at the time of the fire, and now the golden bowl is deposited in the treasury of the people of Clazomenae. It weighs about four hundred forty-five pounds. The bowl stands at the corner of the forecourt of the temple. It will hold the contents of six hundred nine-gallon jars. This is known because the people of Delphi use it to mix wine at the festival called the "Appearance of the Gods," at which the statues of the gods are shown.

In addition, Croesus sent four silver jars with wide mouths, which are in the treasury of the Corinthians, and he dedicated two other vessels which were used for sprinkling water in the rites of purification, at the sacrifices. One of these was of gold, the other of silver.

Along with these, Croesus sent other offerings which were not especially remarkable. In addition, there were some round basins of silver, and a gold statue of a woman, three cubits high. The people of Delphi say that the statue was of the woman who baked for Croesus.

Besides all this, he sent his wife's necklaces and jewelled belts.

These were the gifts that he sent to Delphi. To the shrine of Amphiaraus, since he knew the story of his bravery and of his death, he dedicated a shield of solid gold and a spear made entirely of solid gold; both the point and the shaft were of gold. Both of these were preserved until my time in Thebes, in the Theban temple of Apollo.

To the Lydians who were to bring these gifts to the temples, Croesus gave orders to ask of the oracles

33

whether Croesus should make a campaign against the Persians, and whether he should add to his own army the army of any ally.

When the Lydians arrived at the places to which they had been sent, they offered the gifts, and put the question to the oracles, using these words, "Croesus, king of Lydia and other nations, thinking that here there are the only true oracles among men, presents you with these gifts which you deserve for your wisdom. And now he asks you whether he shall make war against the Persians, and whether he shall add to his force the army of any ally."

This was what they asked, and both oracles agreed in their opinions, and foretold that if Croesus made war against the Persians he would destroy a great empire. They advised him to find out who were the strongest of the Greek states, and bind them to him as his allies.

When these divine sayings were brought back and Croesus learned of them, he was delighted with the oracles and was completely confident that he would destroy the kingdom of Cyrus. He immediately sent to Delphi a present of two gold coins (worth about ten dollars) for every man in Delphi. In return the people of Delphi gave to Croesus and the Lydians the right to consult the oracle ahead of other people, freedom from paying fees, front seats at the official functions, and perpetual citizenship at Delphi for anyone who wished it.

When he made his gifts to the Delphians, Croesus asked a question of the oracle for the third time. Having received one true answer, he was anxious for more.

When he inquired this time, the question he asked was whether he would rule for a long time. The Pythian priestess answered as follows:

When a mule becomes king of the Medes,
Then, tender-footed Lydian, by the stony bed of the
     river Hermus,
Flee and do not wait, and be not ashamed of being
     a coward.

These words pleased Croesus more than any he had heard. He supposed that a mule would never be king of the Medes instead of a man, and he thought that this meant that neither he nor his descendants would ever lose their kingdom.

Then he took careful thought to discover who among the Greeks were strongest, so that he could make them his allies. He made inquiries and found that the Lacedaemonians were the foremost people among the Doric stock, and the Athenians among the Ionic stock.

So Croesus sent messengers with gifts, to the Lacedaemonians in Sparta, to ask for an alliance; and because of the gifts, and because Croesus had invited them to be his allies before he sent to any others, the Lacedaemonians accepted the alliance.

"AS MUCH GOLD AS YOU CAN CARRY"

When the Lydians came from Sardis to consult the oracle at Delphi, a Greek named Alcmaeon helped them very eagerly; and so Croesus, when he heard from the Lydians how this man had assisted them, sent for him to come to Sardis; and when he had come, Croesus said he would make him a present of as much gold as he could carry away on his own body at one time.

So Alcmaeon, when he learned that such was to be the gift, made a plan. He put on a wide tunic and left a deep fold in the front of it and on his feet he put a pair of the widest top-boots he could find; and in this costume he went in to the treasury to which he was led. There he saw a heap of gold dust and fell on it. First of all he poured down alongside his legs all the gold his boots would hold. Then he stuffed the fold of his tunic full of gold and scattered gold dust in his hair and took more of it in his mouth.

And so he came out of the treasury scarcely able to drag his boots along and looking like anything but a man, with his mouth stuffed and his whole body weighted down. When Croesus saw him he was overcome with laughter and made him a present of the gold he was carrying plus the same amount again.

So, then, the family became very rich, and Alcmaeon began to keep four-horse chariots and won prizes with them at the Olympic games.

CROESUS ATTACKS PERSIA

When the proper time came, Croesus led his army toward the Persian territory. In order to reach Persia, the Lydian army had to cross the river Halys. To pass over a large river is not easy for an army, and there are two accounts of how the Lydian army crossed the Halys. I, Herodotus, believe that they crossed the river on the bridges, which were then in existence. But most of the people in Greece believe that the bridges did not yet exist at that time, and that it was Thales of Miletus, one of the Seven Sages and an astronomer and engineer of great wisdom, who got the army across the river. Thales was traveling with the army, and when the Lydians reached the river they made camp. Croesus did not know how the army could get across; but Thales dealt with the problem in the following way. Starting from a point upstream from the camp, he dug a deep trench, along a semicircular line, so that it ran behind the site of the camp and then rejoined the river below the camp. And so the river, turned out of its old bed, was divided into two streams, one in front of the camp, one behind it; and the flow of the water was lowered enough so that both channels could be forded. There are some people, indeed, who say that the old river bed was completely dried up. But this I do not believe; then how could they have crossed the river on the way home?

The Lydians met the Persians at a place near the city of Sinope on the Euxine Sea. There was a sharp battle and many were killed on both sides. By the time night came neither army had the advantage and so they parted.

The Lydian army was much smaller than that of Cyrus, and Croesus saw that if he had had a larger army he would have won. So, since Cyrus did not offer to fight again on the day after the battle, Croesus returned to Sardis and planned to call on the Egyptians and the Babylonians for assistance, because he had alliances with both of them. When all these forces were ready, he planned to wait for the end of winter and march against the Persians when the spring weather made military operations easier. It would take five months for the allies' troops to reach Sardis, so while he was waiting Croesus disbanded all of his hired soldiers who were not Lydians.

After Croesus had left following the battle, Cyrus learned that he planned to disband part of his army. Cyrus understood that the best thing for him was to march as fast as possible to Sardis, before the Lydian army could be assembled again. This he decided and this he did, with speed. He and his army marched into Lydia, and Cyrus brought the news to Croesus himself, before any other word could reach him.

Croesus, then, was in great difficulty, for his affairs had turned out not at all as he had expected. However, he led the Lydian troops out to battle. In those days there was no nation in Asia braver or better at fighting than the Lydians. They fought on horseback and carried long spears, and they managed their horses well.

The armies met in the plain in front of the city of Sardis, which is wide and bare. As Cyrus watched the Lydians drawing up their line of battle, he was afraid—and rightly—of their cavalry; and he adopted a device suggested to him by Harpagus, one of his Persian officers. He collected all the camels that followed the army carrying food and equipment, and took off their loads and mounted upon them men dressed like cavalrymen. Having equipped them in this way, he placed them in front of the rest of his army and gave them orders to advance on Croesus' cavalry. The infantry he ordered to follow the camels, and he put all of his own cavalry behind the infantry.

When he had arranged all of his troops, Cyrus gave an order that they were to kill all the Lydians they met and to spare none of them except Croesus himself; they were not to kill the king even if he tried to defend himself against being captured.

The reason why Cyrus placed the camels in front of the cavalry was this: Horses are afraid of camels and they cannot stand either the sight or the smell of them. And so this was the purpose of his scheme, that Croesus' cavalry, on which the Lydian king counted to win a brilliant victory, should be useless to him. So when they came together in battle, as soon as the Lydian horses smelled the camels and saw them, they turned and ran away, and Croesus' hope was ruined. But the Lydians were not cowards. When they saw what had happened they leaped from their horses and met the Persians on foot. Many were killed on both sides, but at last the Lydians were forced to retreat;

40

and they were driven inside the walls of Sardis and besieged by the Persians.

And so the siege was established. Croesus supposed
that it would last for a long time, and sent another set
of messengers from the city to his allies. The first messengers had been sent to ask them to gather at Sardis
in five months' time; but he sent these to announce that
Croesus was besieged and to ask for help as soon as
possible.

The Spartans were engaged in a war with the people
of Argos when the news came that Croesus was being
besieged. Nevertheless, when they heard the herald's
message, they prepared to give help. But when they
had collected their equipment and the ships were ready,
another messenger arrived, saying that the city of the
Lydians was taken and that Croesus was prisoner. And
so, though they were greatly saddened by the news,
they gave up their plan.

Sardis was taken in this way: When it had been
fourteen days since Croesus was besieged, Cyrus sent
horsemen to ride about through his army to promise
rewards to the man who should be the first to mount
the wall of the city. After this, the army tried an as-
sault, but it came to nothing. Then, when the army had
come to a stop, a man of the nomad tribe of the Mardi,
Hyroeades by name, undertook to go up at a part of
the citadel where there was no guard. There was no
guard because the fortification wall was so steep here

that it was thought that no one could attack it. But this Mardian, Hyroeades, on the day before had watched one of the Lydians climb down this part of the wall to fetch a helmet which had fallen down the slope. Hyroeades watched this and thought about it. Then he climbed up and other Persians followed him. A number of them made the ascent, and so the whole city was on the point of being sacked.

This is what happened to Croesus himself: He had a son, who was a fine young man except that he was dumb. In his days of prosperity Croesus had done everything he could for him. He thought of everything that could be done, and had also sent to Delphi to inquire of the oracle concerning him. The Pythian priestess at the oracle answered in these words:

> O Lydian, king of many men, Croesus, you are very
>   foolish.
> Do not wish to hear the voice of your son in the
>   palace.
> It would be better for you if he remained as he is.
> The day when you first hear him speaking will be un-
>   lucky.

When the fortress was being taken, one of the Persians, not knowing Croesus, came at him to kill him. Croesus saw the man coming upon him, but his misfortune had put him past caring, and it would not matter to him if he were struck down and killed. But his son, who was dumb, when he saw the Persian coming, broke into speech in his fear and grief, and called out, "Don't you kill Croesus!" This was the first time he spoke, and after that for the rest of his life he was able to speak.

CROESUS ON THE PYRE

So the Persians captured Sardis and made Croesus prisoner. He had reigned for fourteen years and had been besieged for fourteen days. When the Persians seized him they took him to Cyrus. Cyrus built a great pyre and bound Croesus in chains and set him on it, along with twice seven Lydian boys. Either he intended to sacrifice them as first fruits to one of his gods, or he wished to fulfill a vow he had made, or perhaps he had learned that Croesus was a god-fearing man and it was for this reason that he set him up on the pyre, hoping to discover whether any of the gods would rescue him from being burned alive.

This was what Cyrus did; and as for Croesus, even though he was standing on the pyre, in such an evil

43

situation, there came to his mind the thought that that saying of Solon's had truly been inspired by heaven; namely, that no living man is to be considered blessed. He had not spoken a word when this thought came to him; but now he sighed deeply and groaned and said, "Solon! Solon! Solon!" Cyrus heard this, and ordered his interpreters to ask Croesus who this was that he was calling upon. The interpreters came near Croesus and questioned him. At first when they asked him, Croesus kept silent; but after a while when he was forced to answer, he said, "I would have given a great deal of my wealth if all sovereigns could have conversed with him."

What he said was obscure to them, and again they asked him the meaning of what he was saying. When they urged him and pressed him to answer, he told them how Solon, an Athenian, once came to Sardis, and after he had seen all Croesus' treasure he had taken it lightly, saying various things about it; and he told them how everything had happened to him just as Solon said it would, though Solon spoke more with reference to mankind in general, and especially those who considered themselves fortunate, than concerning Croesus.

While Croesus was telling the story, the pyre had already been lit and was burning around the edges. But Cyrus, when he heard from the interpreters what Croesus said, repented of what he had done. It came to his mind that he, a human being, was putting into the fire, alive, another human being, who had been no less fortunate than himself. In addition, he began to fear divine punishment, and he realized that there was nothing stable in men's affairs. So he gave the order to put out the burning fire as quickly as possible and to bring Croesus and those with him down from the pyre. But the servants, try as they could, were not able to get the fire under control.

Then, the people of Lydia relate, when Croesus understood that Cyrus had repented, and saw that all the people were trying to put out the fire but were not able to bring it under control, he cried out and called on Apollo, praying that if the god had ever been pleased with any of his gifts, he would come to his aid and save him from the evil which pressed upon him. Thus Croesus called on the god, with tears; and suddenly, in a clear sky with no wind, clouds gathered and a storm burst and it began to rain, the most violent kind of rain, and the pyre was put out.

CROESUS
AND CYRUS

From this Cyrus understood that Croesus was a good man, favored by the gods, and he brought him down from the pyre and questioned him as follows, "Croesus, who persuaded you to invade my country and be my enemy instead of my friend?"

"O King," Croesus answered, "I did this myself, and brought good fortune to you and ill fortune to myself. But the cause of it all was the god of the Greeks, the oracle at Delphi, who encouraged me to make the campaign. No one is foolish enough to prefer war to peace. In peace, sons bury their fathers, but in war, fathers bury their sons. But it must have been the will of heaven that these things should happen thus."

So spoke Croesus, and Cyrus released him and made him sit beside him and began to think about him earnestly; and Cyrus and all his people who were with him looked upon Croesus with wonder. But Croesus was lost in thought and sat in silence. After a while he turned about, and when he saw the Persians sacking the city of the Lydians, he said, "O King, shall I tell you now what I am thinking or must I be silent?"

Cyrus bade him say boldly whatever he would. Croesus asked him, "That great crowd of people, what are they doing so eagerly?"

Cyrus replied, "They are plundering your city and carrying off your wealth."

But Croesus answered, "No, not my city or my wealth, for this is no longer mine; it is your wealth that they are carrying off."

Cyrus began to think carefully about what Croesus said, and he ordered the people around them to withdraw and asked Croesus what he thought about what he, Cyrus, was doing.

Croesus said, "Since the gods have given me to you as a slave, I think it is my duty, if I can give you any advice, to give it to you. The Persians are proud by nature; and they are also poor. If you allow them to seize great wealth, and keep it, this is what you must expect will happen: The one who has got the most money will rebel against you. Now do this, if what I say seems right to you: Take men from your guard and put them on duty at every gate, and have them take away the spoils from the people who are carrying them out of the city, and have them tell the people that they must pay tribute to Zeus. In this way you will not be hated when you take away their loot, and they will admit that you are acting justly and will give up their loot willingly."

When Cyrus heard this he was delighted, for he thought the advice was well said. He praised Croesus warmly and ordered his guards to do what Croesus had advised; and he said to Croesus, "Croesus, though you are a king, you have made up your mind to serve me and to speak nobly. Ask me for whatever gift you wish, and it will be given to you at once."

Croesus said, "Master, you will please me most if you allow me to send these chains to that god of the Greeks to whom I chiefly paid honor and to ask him whether it is his custom to disappoint those who serve him well."

Cyrus asked him what this request meant, and Croesus repeated to him the story of his own plan and the answers of the oracles; and he described his own offerings to the gods, and told how it was the oracle that had encouraged him to make the campaign against the Persians. After he had described all this he once more requested permission to reproach the god.

Cyrus laughed and said, "This you shall obtain from me, Croesus, and everything that you may ever ask of me."

When Croesus heard this, he sent some of the Lydians to Delphi and bade them lay his chains upon the doorstep of the temple, and ask whether the god were not ashamed of having advised Croesus to make war on the Persians and of having told him that he would destroy the power of Cyrus. They were to show the chains and say that they were the first fruits of that advice. This is what they were to ask of the god; and they were to inquire whether it was the custom of the Greek gods not to return favors to those who worshipped them.

When the Lydians arrived, and said what they had been commanded to say, the priestess—as the account goes—spoke as follows. "It is impossible for any man to escape his destined fate. Not even is this possible for a god. Croesus had paid in full for the sin of his ancestor in the fifth generation. It was the desire of Apollo that the punishment of Sardis should take place in the time of the sons of Croesus, and not in Croesus' own lifetime; but he could not divert the Fates from their course. But so far as they would give way to him, he showed favor to Croesus. He delayed the capture of Sardis for three years. Let Croesus know that even if he is a captive, it is so many years later than what was first decreed. Furthermore, the god came to his rescue when he was on the pyre. But as for the oracle that was given to him, it is not right for Croesus to complain. What the god predicted to him was that if he led his army against the Persians, he would destroy a great empire. If he were taking careful thought, he should have sent to ask whether the god meant his own empire or that of Cyrus. But he did not understand what was said and he did not ask any further questions; so let him blame himself alone. When he asked that final question, and the god gave him that answer concerning the mule, even this he did not understand. Cyrus was the mule. He was the son of two people who did not belong to the same nation. The mother was of better rank, the father of inferior origin. She was a Median, daughter of Astyages, the king of the Medians. He was a Persian and under the rule of the Medians, and he was married to one who should have been his sovereign queen."

This was what the priestess answered to the Lydians. They took the answer to Sardis and reported it to Croesus. When he heard it, he confessed that the sin was his own, not the god's.

This is how it was with the reign of Croesus.

Darius, King of Persia

DARIUS WAS THE SON of Hystaspes, who had been governor of one of the provinces in Persia. A man named Gaumata had managed to seize the Persian throne, and several of the notable men in Persia formed a plot to get rid of him. Darius joined them, and they killed the usurper in the palace. Darius thus became the successor of Cyrus.

Darius was an able and active monarch, ambitious to extend his power beyond the Hellespont and into Europe. He actually crossed the Hellespont with his army and marched as far as the Danube, and one of his generals, Megabazus, occupied Thrace in the northern part of Greece.

A little after this, when Darius had returned to his capital, Susa, some of the leaders of the Greek cities along the coast of Asia Minor, which had been subject to the Persian king, planned a revolt. The Athenians decided to help their fellow Greeks, and sent a fleet of twenty warships to the assistance of the rebels in Asia Minor. The sending of this fleet was the beginning of trouble for both the Greeks and the Persians.

The Greek forces, including the Athenians and the Eretrians, captured and burned Sardis, and the destruction of the city was such a blow to Darius' pride that he gave orders to one of his servants to say to him three times, every time he sat down to dinner, "Master, remember the Athenians."

THE FIRST INVASION OF GREECE

Darius suppressed the revolt of the Greeks in Asia Minor, and then began to organize an invasion of Greece, to punish the Athenians and the other Greeks.

When Darius was satisfied that his army was ready, he went over the heads of all his other generals, and appointed a young man named Mardonius commander of the force. Mardonius proceeded to march to the coast with a very large army. The Persian fleet was waiting off the coast, and Mardonius went on board ship and set sail toward the Hellespont, leaving other generals to march the troops to the Hellespont.

So there gathered at the Hellespont an enormous force of ships and men. The troops were ferried across the strait in the ships and Mardonius began his march through Greece. His main objectives were Athens and Eretria, which had joined Athens in helping the Greeks in Asia Minor. But the Persians actually intended to destroy as many Greek cities as they could.

53

The fleet sailed across from the Hellespont and followed the army along the coast. When the fleet reached the promontory of Athos and began to sail around it, the ships were caught in a violent gale blowing from the north and many of them were driven ashore on Athos. It is said that three hundred ships were destroyed and over twenty thousand men were lost. The sea around Athos is full of man-eating creatures and many of the Persians were seized and eaten by these. Others were dashed against the rocks and crushed. Some did not know how to swim, and others perished of cold in the water.

While the fleet was suffering this disaster, Mardonius and the troops were attacked in their camp one night by a Thracian tribe. The Thracians killed many of them, and wounded Mardonius himself.

This was the end of the campaign, and Mardonius was forced to retreat to Asia in disgrace.

Darius' servant continued to remind his master of the Athenians. Because of his failure on the previous expedition, he relieved Mardonius of his command and appointed two other generals to lead the expedition against Eretria and Athens, namely Datis, who was a Median, and Artaphernes, Darius' nephew. Darius gave them orders to go and make slaves of the people of Athens and Eretria, and to bring the captives back for him to see.

These new generals left the court and went to the

plain along the coast of Cilicia, taking with them a large force of men, well equipped. When they encamped in Cilicia the naval force joined them. These were the ships and men that the subject states had been ordered to supply, plus the cavalry transports that Darius the year before had commanded the tributary states to furnish.

When the horses had been put on board the cavalry transports and the troops on the other ships, they set sail for the Ionian coast, a fleet of six hundred triremes. When they reached Ionia they did not sail along the coast toward the Hellespont and Thrace, but set out from the island of Samos and sailed through the Aegean islands, I suppose because the generals feared the passage around Athos, which the year before had resulted in such a great disaster.

Another reason for doing this was the island of Naxos, which had not been captured in the former expedition. When the fleet approached Naxos, the people of the city fled to the hills. The Persians captured some of them, to make slaves of them, and burned the city and its temples. Then they sailed away to attack the other islands.

While the Persians were doing this, the people of the sacred island of Delos fled to another island, Tenos. As the Persian fleet was bearing down on Delos, Datis went on ahead, and would not let the ships anchor at Delos, but sent them off to an island opposite. Then he found out where the people of Delos were, and sent a herald to them with the following message:

"Men of the sacred island, why have you not understood what kind of person I am? Instead you have gone away and abandoned your sacred home. I surely have sense enough by myself, even if the king had not given me orders, to do no harm to the place in which the two gods, Apollo and Artemis, were born—no harm either to the soil or to the people. Now come back to your homes and continue to dwell in your own island."

After he had sent this message, he piled on the altar three hundred talents' weight of frankincense, about 18,000 pounds, and burned this as an offering to the gods. When he had done this, Datis sailed with his army against Eretria, taking with him a number of Ionians and Aeolians.

After he had left and put out to sea, Delos was shaken by an earthquake. The people of Delos said this was the first and only earthquake before my time. It may be that this was a sign sent from heaven as a warning of the troubles that were coming to mankind. In three reigns—those of Darius, son of Hystaspes; Xerxes, son of Darius; and Artoxerxes, son of Xerxes —more evils came to Greece than in the six hundred years before Darius.

These troubles came in part from the Persians and in part from the wars which the principal city-states carried on among themselves as they contended for the

56

supreme leadership. So it was not at all unusual that Delos should suffer an earthquake when it had been free from earthquakes previously. In fact, there was an oracle concerning Delos in which this was written:

And I shall shake Delos, though it never before had been shaken.

And in Greek, these are the meanings of the names of the kings I mentioned: Darius means The Doer, Xerxes means The Warrior, Artoxerxes The Great Warrior. And that is what the Greeks could rightly call these kings in their own language.

The foreigners put out to sea from Delos and went around to the other islands, and took men for their army from them, and made hostages of the young sons of the islanders. When, as they sailed around among the islands, they came to Carystos, the Carystians would not either give them hostages, or join them against Eretria and Athens; and so the Persians besieged them and ruined their fields, till the Carystians gave themselves up to the Persians' demands.

The Eretrians, when they learned that the Persian force was sailing toward them, begged the Athenians to come to their assistance. The Athenians did not refuse their help, but sent them for their defense four thousand tenant farmers. But the Eretrians had no sound plan, even though they sent to the Athenians for aid, and they had different ideas among themselves. Some of them wished to abandon the city and flee to the heights of the island of Euboea. Others were plotting to betray the city in the hope of gaining profit for themselves from the Persans. Then Aeschines, the son of Nothon, who was one of the leading men in the city, learning how matters stood in both parties, told the state of affairs to the Athenians who had come, and begged them to leave and return to their own country, lest they be destroyed along with the others. The Athenians followed the advice of Aeschines.

The Persians arrived at the territory of Eretria and took possesion of some small towns; and then they disembarked their horses and prepared to attack the city of Eretria itself. But the Eretrians had no intention of coming out and fighting. All they were concerned about was to guard the walls.

The Persians made a stout attack on the walls, and for six days many fell on both sides: but on the seventh day two men of good standing in the city, Euphorbus, son of Alcimachus, and Philagrus, son of Cineas, betrayed it to the Persians. So these entered the city and pillaged the temples and set fire to them, in revenge for the temples that had been burned in Sardis; and following Darius' command they made slaves of the townspeople.

THE PERSIANS MOVE ON MARATHON

Having conquered Eretria, they paused for a few days and then sailed for Attica, pressing on energetically and thinking that they would do to the Athenians what they had done to the Eretrians. Since the plain of Marathon was the part of Attica that was most suited for cavalry action, and also nearest to Eretria, they were guided thither by Hippias, son of Pisistratus.

This Hippias and his younger brother Hipparchus had succeeded their father Pisistratus, who had been tyrant of Athens. They continued their father's policy in the rule of the city, but Hipparchus, because of his personal misconduct, was murdered by two patriotic Athenians, Harmodius and Aristogiton. After his brother's death, Hippias became harsh and was finally driven out of Athens. He went to the court of Darius and accompanied the invasion army, hoping to get revenge on the Athenians for their treatment of him.

When the Athenians learned of the Persians' movements, they, too, hurried to Marathon. According to their custom, they were commanded by ten generals, of whom the tenth was Miltiades. He had had an active and adventurous career in which he had showed great ability and daring, and he had been elected by popular vote along with all the other generals.

THE RUN OF PHIDIPPIDES

While they were still in Athens, the generals sent the news to Sparta, using as herald Phidippides the Athenian, a long distance runner who made it his profession to carry messages in this way. As Phidippides himself related and reported to the Athenians, the god Pan met him while he was in the Parthenian hills above Tegea. He said that Pan called him by name and commanded him to say to the Athenians, "Why do you pay no attention to me, though I have been your friend, and have often been of service to you, and will be again in the future?"

The Athenians believed that what Phidippides said

was true, and when their affairs were in a prosperous condition, they founded a temple to Pan below the Acropolis, and as a result of that message, they endeavored to win the god's favor with annual sacrifices and torch races.

But on this occasion—that is, when Phidippides was sent by the generals and reported that he saw Pan—he reached Sparta on the day after he left Athens. The distance was about one hundred fifty miles. He came before the rulers and said, "Men of Sparta, the Athenians beg you to send them help and not to allow a most ancient city of Hellas to be enslaved by barbarians. For Eretria has already been enslaved, and Hellas is weaker by the loss of an important city."

So Phidippides gave the message that had been entrusted to him, and the Spartans were glad to send help to the Athenians; but it was impossible for them to do this immediately, for they did not wish to break their law. It was the ninth day from the beginning of the month, and they could not set out on an expedition—so they said—on the ninth day, when the moon was not full.

And so the Spartans waited for the full moon, and Hippias, the son of Pisistratus, led the Persians to Marathon. On the way, Hippias, being now the guide of the expedition, advised the Persians to leave the Eretrian captives under guard on the island of Aeglea.

The night before they arrived at Marathon, Hippias

had a dream which he took to mean that he would return to Athens, regain his power, and die as an old man in his own country. It was he who arranged the way in which the ships anchored when they came to the bay of Marathon, and drew up the Persians in battle formation when they came off the ships.

It happened that while Hippias was doing this, he was seized with an unusually violent fit of sneezing and coughing. Since he was an old man, most of his teeth were loose; and he coughed so violently that one of them fell out. It fell into the sand and he tried hard to find it; but it was nowhere to be seen, and Hippias said with a groan to the people who were with him, "This is not our land, and we shall not be able to conquer it. By falling out, my tooth has shown this; for it is a part of me, and it has demonstrated that it has occupied all of the land that was to be my share."

THE BATTLE AT
MARATHON

The Athenians were drawn up in battle order on a piece of land that was sacred to Heracles, and now the whole army of the city of Plataea came to their aid. The Athenian generals had different opinions as to what should be done. Some would not consent to a battle because they maintained that the army was too small to fight with the Persians, while others argued that they should give battle. Miltiades was one of the latter. While they were arguing, and it seemed that the more cautious policy was winning, there was an eleventh man who had a vote, namely the Athenian who had been chosen polemarch—that is, War Archon—by lot. By an old custom, the Athenians gave the polemarch a vote among the generals. On this occasion the polemarch was Callimachus of Aphidnae; and Miltiades went to him and said this:

"Callimachus, it is in your power today either to cause Athens to be enslaved or to make her free and thereby leave a memory, throughout the whole future history of mankind, such as not even Harmodius and Aristogiton left. The people of Athens are now in the greatest danger they have been in since they existed. If they bow themselves in surrender to the Persians, they know what will happen, for they will be turned over to Hippias. But if the city is able to overcome this danger, it is capable of becoming the first of the cities of the Greeks.

"Let me tell you how this can be, and how it happens that you are the one who can decide. We, the ten generals, are divided into two parties. Some are urging a battle, some are against it. If we do not fight, I believe that a great division of opinion will fall upon the Athenian people, and upset their thinking until they decide to make friends with the Persians. But if we go into battle before any corrupt idea takes possession of the Athenians, then, if the gods see to it that there is fair play, we are capable of winning the battle. All these things have come together on you and they all depend on you. If you add yourself to my party, your native soil will be free and your city will be the first in Hellas. But if you choose the opinion of those who are eager not to fight, you will get the opposite of the good things I have spoken of."

What Miltiades said won Callimachus to his way of thinking, and when the polemarch's vote was added, the decision was to fight. It was the custom for each general in turn to have the supreme command for one day; and each of the generals who had voted to fight, when his day came offered his own turn to Miltiades. Miltiades received each of these offers, but would not begin the battle until his own turn came.

When the command came to Miltiades, the Athenians were drawn up for battle in the following way. The right wing was commanded by the polemarch Callimachus, for at that time it was the custom among the Athenians for the polemarch to have the right wing. Callimachus being the leader in that place, next to him there were drawn up the tribes of the city, standing next to each other in their numerical order. Finally the Plataeans were drawn up on the left wing. Beginning from the time of that battle, when the Athenians bring sacrifices to the festivals that are celebrated every five years, such as the Panathenaea—the birthday of Athens— and the festival of Poseidon, the Athenian herald prays that good things may come to both the Athenians and the Plataeans.

But while the Athenians were being drawn up at Marathon, it turned out that when their line was arranged so that it was the same length as the Persian army, the center was only a few ranks deep, and here was the weakest part of the line, for each of the wings was quite strong.

So when they were drawn up in order, and the customary sacrifices had been made and had produced favorable omens, the Athenians were given the word and began to charge the barbarians on the run. The space between the armies was not less than a mile. When the Persians saw them coming on the run, they prepared to receive the Athenians. The barbarians thought the Athenians were mad, rushing to their own destruction, for there were so few of them and yet they were charging on the run, without the support of cavalry or archers.

This is what the Persians imagined; but the Athenians, when they had all closed with the barbarians, fought in a way to be remembered. They were the first Greeks, so far as I know, who charged against the enemy at a run; and they were the first who could actually stand the sight of the Persian dress and of the men who were in it. Until that time, even the name of the Persians had frightened the Greeks.

The fighting at Marathon lasted for a long time. The barbarians defeated the center of the line, where the Persians and the Sacae were stationed. Here the barbarians won and broke the line and pursued the Greeks inland. But on each of the wings the Athenians and the Plataeans won. When they had got the upper hand, they did not pursue the barbarians whom they had put to flight, but drew together their two wings and fought with the barbarians who had broken their center; and here the Athenians were victorious. As the Persians fled, the Athenians pursued them and cut them down, until they came to the sea. Here they called for fire and laid hold of the ships.

It was in this work that the polemarch Callimachus was killed, after he had proved himself a brave man. One of the generals died there as well, Stesilaus, son of Thrasylaus. Likewise Cynegirus, son of Euphorion, fell there, his hand cut off by an axe as he seized one of the ships; and many other famous Athenians fell.

In this way the Athenians captured seven ships. In those that were left the Persians pushed off from the beach. They took the Eretrian captives from the island where they had left them, and sailed round Sunium, hoping to reach Athens before the Athenian troops. People accused the members of the noble family of the Alcmeonidae of thinking of this device. It was said that they had made an agreement with the Persians and gave them a signal by raising a shield when they had got back to their ships.

While the Persians were sailing round Sunium, the Athenians returned to the city as fast as their feet could carry them, and they arrived before the barbarians did. Having come from one place sacred to Heracles in Marathon, they made camp in another plot of ground sacred to Heracles, this being the gymnasium called Cynosarges, outside the city. The barbarian fleet waited for a while off Phalerum, which was then the naval harbor of Athens, and after they had waited there for a while at anchor they sailed back to Asia.

In this fight at Marathon about 6,400 barbarians died, while of the Athenians 192 were killed.

The Spartans came to Athens two thousand strong after the full moon—though they hurried so that they reached Attica on the third day after leaving Sparta. Though they came too late for the battle, they asked to see the dead Persians; and they went to Marathon and saw them. After that, praising the Athenians and their deeds, they went home.

The Second Invasion of Greece

DARIUS' PREPARATIONS

THE NEWS OF THE BATTLE at Marathon came to Darius. He was already exceedingly angry with the Greeks because of their attack on Sardis. Now he was much more wrathful and even more determined to continue war with Greece. He immediately sent messengers to all his cities commanding them to prepare an army. Each city was required to furnish even more than it had previously in the way of warships and horses, food and transports.

This was the command that went round. The whole of Asia was in a turmoil for three years. The best men were enrolled for the campaign against Greece and the preparations went ahead.

In the fourth year, the Egyptians, who were subject to the Persians, revolted. At that, Darius determined to send expeditions against both Greece and Egypt.

When the two expeditions were being made ready, a great quarrel arose among Darius' sons concerning the succession to the throne. According to Persian law, a king may not set out on an expedition without naming his heir. Before he became king, Darius had three sons by his first wife, and then after he became king, he had four more sons by his queen Atossa. Artobazanes was the eldest of the earlier sons; Xerxes was the eldest of those who came later. Being of different mothers, they were rivals; but it was Xerxes who was able to persuade Darius to declare him next in succession, on the ground that he was the first to be born after his father became king.

Darius continued his preparations, but a year later death came to him, after he had reigned thirty-six years; and so he was never able to punish either the Greeks or the Egyptians.

XERXES
BECOMES KING

So on Darius' death the power went to his son Xerxes. At first Xerxes was not at all interested in undertaking a campaign against Greece. Instead he began to collect forces to go against Egypt. But there was a man who had great influence with him, his cousin Mardonius, son of Darius' sister. Mardonius persuaded Xerxes that he could not let the Greeks escape punishment for what they had done to the Persians; and he praised Greece, saying that it was a fine country, worthy of having Xerxes as its king. Mardonius himself was eager for adventures, and hoped that he would be Xerxes' viceroy in Greece. There were factions in Greece itself that sent to Xerxes and offered to aid the Persians. So Xerxes was persuaded. In the year following Darius' death, he set out against the Egyptian rebels and brought them back into slavery, and made their condition much harsher than it had been under Darius.

71

XERXES' ARMY

After the subjugation of Egypt, Xerxes spent four whole years preparing his army and the supplies for it. Before the end of the fifth year he set out with a great multitude of men. Of all the armies that we know of, this was by far the greatest. No other army was anything in comparison with it.

There was no nation in Asia that did not form a part of this army that Xerxes was leading against Greece. Only the greatest rivers were large enough to supply water for the army to drink. Some nations furnished ships, others were enlisted as infantry. Some supplied cavalry transports to follow the army, others furnished warships which could form bridges. Others again provided food and other kinds of ships.

THE CANAL
AT ATHOS

Since the first Persians who had tried to sail around Athos had been shipwrecked, Xerxes had spent three years preparing to deal with the situation there. Some triremes were anchored near the peninsula, and from these, men of all the kinds that composed the army were to be sent to Athos and set to work digging a canal, taking turns at the work, and laboring under the lash. The people who lived on Athos also worked at the digging.

Athos is a great and famous mountain, projecting into the sea. It is inhabited. At the land side, where the mountain ends, it has the form of a peninsula, and there is an isthmus about a mile and a half wide. From one shore to the other the ground is level or has only small hills. There were some Greek towns on the isthmus and elsewhere on Athos.

As they dug, the barbarians divided up the work among the nations who were represented in the army.

73

They drew a straight line, and when the canal had been dug to some depth, some stayed at the bottom and dug, while others took the earth as fast as it was dug and passed it on to their comrades who were standing above them on steps cut out of the earth, till it reached those at the top, who carried it away and dumped it.

With every one of the national groups, save that of the Phoenicians, the sides of the canal, being steep, broke and fell from time to time, and so made double work when the sides had to be dug out again. Since they made the excavation the same width at the top and the bottom, something like this was bound to happen. But the Phoenicians here showed the same cleverness that they display in everything else. When they took over the portion that fell to them, they made the top of the excavation twice as wide as the canal was to be. As they dug down, they narrowed the excavation in proportion; and when they came to the bottom, their excavation was the same width as the work of the other nations. There was a field near by in which a market place was set so that the men could go there and make purchases. Ground grain was regularly brought to them from Asia.

As I think about it, it seems to me that it was out of pride that Xerxes commanded this canal to be dug, because he wished to demonstrate his power and leave a memorial of it. It would have been possible without much trouble to haul the ships overland across the isthmus; but he ordered a canal to be dug to let in the sea, wide enough so that two triremes could pass through it side by side.

The same men who were in charge of the digging were also ordered to put a bridge across the Strymon River. For material for the bridges he instructed the Phoenicians and the Egyptians to make ropes, some of papyrus, some of flax. He commanded the same people to establish at intervals stores of food for the army, so that neither the soldiers nor the animals should suffer from hunger as they marched on Greece. He had inquiries made as to the places where it would be best to store the food, and then had it brought from all parts of Asia in merchant vessels and transports.

While all these people carried out the tasks that had been laid on them, the whole of the land force had been collected and was marching on Sardis, Xerxes with it, starting out from the point in Cappadocia which had been designated as the collecting point for the force which was to march with Xerxes by land. Which of the territorial governors received the gifts that had been promised by the king for bringing the best equipped army, I cannot say: I am not sure that the matter was ever decided.

When Xerxes reached Sardis, he first of all sent heralds to Greece to demand the gift of earth and water which was a sign of submission and to order that meals be prepared for the king. He did not demand earth of Athens or Sparta. The reason why he sent to ask for earth and water a second time was that he thought that those who had not given it to Darius, when he sent his messengers, would now send the gifts to him through fear. It was because he wished to make sure of this that he now sent his heralds.

BRIDGING THE HELLESPONT

After he had done this he made ready to march to Abydos. In the meantime his people had been building a bridge across the Hellespont between Asia and Europe. On the Chersonese, which forms the European side of the Hellespont, there is a broad headland running out into the sea opposite Abydos. So the men whose task it was to do this work started out from Abydos and built bridges passing over to join this headland. The Egyptians built one bridge with cables of flax; the Phoenicians built another with papyrus cables. The distance from Abydos to the opposite shore was a little less than a mile.

But as soon as the strait had been bridged, a great storm fell upon it and broke up and scattered all the work that had been done. Xerxes, when he heard of this, was exceedingly angry and commanded that the Hellespont be beaten with three hundred lashes and that a pair of fetters be thrown into it. Indeed I have heard that he sent along men who branded cattle and slaves, to brand the Hellespont with hot irons. What is certain is that he ordered his people, as they scourged the Hellespont, to speak these strange and arrogant words: "You bitter stream, our master lays this punishment upon you because he suffered wrong from you, although he had done you no injury. Indeed Xerxes, the king, will pass over you whether you wish it or not. But it is right that no man should offer you sacrifice, for you are a stormy and briny river." This was the way in which he commanded that the sea be punished; and he ordered that those who had been in charge of building the bridges should have their heads cut off.

This was what was done by the men to whom that troublesome honor came; and other engineers set about the task of bridging the stream. They constructed their bridges in the following way. To lighten the strain on the cables, they lashed together galleys and triremes to support the two bridges. The bridge that was in the direction of the Euxine Sea was carried on 360 ships; the other bridge was carried by 314. The ships were drawn up so that they lay parallel with the current and at right angles to the bridges which they supported. Heavy anchors were put out from the end of each ship in the direction of the Pontus, to hold the ship against the wind that blew from that quarter, and similar anchors were put out from the other end, toward the west and the Aegean Sea, to hold the ship against the winds which blew from the west and south. They left an opening for passage between the ships so that anyone who wished to sail into the Pontus or out of it might be able to do so.

When the vessels had been drawn up in position, they pulled the cables taut, twisting them by means of wooden windlasses mounted on the shore. They did not, as with the first bridges, use the two kinds of cables separately, but they employed for each bridge two cables of flax and four of papyrus. These were all of the same thickness and very fine in appearance; but the flaxen cables were heavier in relation to their size. A length of about twenty inches of such cable weighed about eighty pounds.

After the bridge had been carried over the strait, they sawed planks of wood equal in length to the length of the ships and placed them on top of the taut cables. Then they joined the planks side by side and fastened them together. After this they brought brushwood to the bridge and when this was laid down in order they spread earth on top of the brushwood and tamped it down. Then they made a fence on either side of each bridge, so that the baggage animals and the cavalry horses might not be frightened when they saw the sea below them.

The work at Athos was finished, including the two breakwaters at the entrances of the canal which were designed to keep the surf from filling up the entrances with silt; and so the canal was reported to be completely ready. And when the bridges were finished, the army, after having spent the winter at Sardis, set out at the beginning of spring and marched toward Abydos.

When the army set out, the sun left its normal position in the heavens and was not seen, though there were no clouds and the sky was clear, and instead of day it was night. When Xerxes saw this he wondered what it signified and asked the Magians what this strange sight meant. They assured him that the god was foretelling to the Greeks the eclipse of their cities, for the sun, they said, was the body which proclaimed future events to the Greeks, just as the moon did for the Persians. Xerxes was delighted to hear this and pressed on with his march.

THE MARCHING ORDER OF THE PERSIANS

First went the baggage and the pack animals, and, after them, a mixed force of all kinds of peoples all thrown together and not kept separate and in order. When more than half this crowd had passed, a space was left, so that these people should not come into contact with the king.

Ahead of the king there came, first, a thousand picked horsemen, the finest that could be found among all the Persians. After these came a thousand spearmen, all picked men like the others. They carried their spears reversed, pointing toward the ground. Then came ten of the sacred horses of the great Nisaean plain in Media, which produces horses of unusual size. Behind these ten horses came the sacred chariot of Zeus, whom the Persians know under the name of Ormuzd. This was drawn by eight white horses and the charioteer followed the horses on foot, holding the reins, for no mortal man may ride in this seat of Zeus.

After these came Xerxes in a chariot drawn by Nisaean horses, his charioteer standing beside him.

This was the way Xerxes went out of Sardis; but whenever he wished a change, he would leave the chariot and ride in a carriage. Behind him came a thousand spearmen, the best and more highly born of the Persians, carrying their spears in the usual fashion. After them marched another thousand picked horsemen, and after the horsemen, ten thousand on foot, picked men from the rest of the Persians. A thousand of these carried shafts tipped with golden pomegranates instead of spears. These surrounded the rest of the spearmen, and the nine thousand who were within carried silver pomegranates. Those who held their spears reversed carried golden pomegranates, and those that were closest to Xerxes carried apples of gold. After these ten thousand, came ten thousand Persian horsemen. After these horsemen, there was a gap of a quarter of a mile, and then came the rest of the ordinary soldiers all mixed up together.

When Xerxes had arrived at Abydos, he wished to review his army. A marble throne had been prepared for this purpose, on a hill. The people of Abydos had got this ready ahead of time at the king's command. Xerxes sat there and looked down on his army and his ships at the seashore; and as he looked at them he was seized with a desire to see a race of the ships. When they held the race, the Phoenicians of Sidon won it;

and Xerxes took pleasure in the race and in his forces.

Then, as he saw the whole Hellespont hidden with his ships, and all the beaches and fields of the region of Abydos completely filled with his men, Xerxes first declared that he was blessed, and then began to weep. His uncle Artabanus asked why he wept, after having asserted that he was so happy. Xerxes replied, "As I was thinking about these things, I was overcome with sadness at the thought of how short a man's life is. Out of all these men—and there are so many of them—not one will be living a hundred years from now."

CROSSING
THE HELLESPONT

They spent the whole day making preparations for the crossing, and the next day they waited until they saw the sun rise. Then they burned all kinds of incense on the bridges and strewed the roadways of the bridges with myrtle boughs. As the sun came up, Xerxes poured an offering of wine out of a flat wooden bowl, and, turning toward the sun, prayed that no misfortune might come to stop him before he had conquered Europe and advanced to its farthest borders. When he had finished the prayer, he cast the bowl into the Hellespont, and along with it a large golden bowl used for mixing water and wine, and a Persian sword. I am not able to say certainly whether he cast these into the sea as an offering to the sun, or whether he was sorry for having scourged the Hellespont and gave these gifts to the sea to show that he was sorry.

When all this was done, they made the crossing. The foot soldiers and the cavalry went over the bridge on the side toward the Pontus, and the baggage animals and the equipment passed over the bridge on the side toward the Aegean. First came the ten thousand Persians, all wearing wreaths, and after them the mixed force made up of all kinds of nations. It took these the whole of the first day to cross, and on the next day first came the horsemen and those who carried their spears reversed; these, too, wore wreaths. After them crossed the sacred horses and the sacred chariot, and after these Xerxes himself and the spear-bearers and the thousand horsemen; and after these came the rest of the army. At the same time the ships that were not being used to support the bridge crossed over to the opposite shore.

When Xerxes crossed over to the European shore,

he watched his army crossing, driven along under the whips. The army spent seven days and seven nights in the crossing, with no time allowed for rest.

THE PERSIAN ARMY

The army then set out on its march, while the fleet sailed ahead. On this part of the march Xerxes stopped to count his army. There seems to be no record of the size of each section of the army, but the total was 1,700,100 men. They were counted in this way: They collected ten thousand men in one place and packed them together as closely as possible. Then they drew a line around them on the ground. The ten thousand men were then sent away and a stone wall was built around the area, to the height of a man's waist. Then they brought others into the walled enclosure until all were numbered in this way. When they had been counted, they were divided up according to nationalities.

The Persians were equipped as follows: They wore

loose caps called tiaras; tunics with sleeves, of various colors; coats of mail, made of iron scales like those of fish; and trousers. Instead of metal shields they carried wicker ones, with their quivers hanging below them. They carried short spears, heavy bows, and arrows made of reeds, and wore daggers hanging from their belts, over the right thigh. All the other nations wore their characteristic clothing and carried various kinds of weapons. For example, some wore bronze helmets, some had caps made of fox skins. Some wore leather tunics.

The ten thousand Persians who were called The Immortals were splendidly equipped. They were called Immortals because if any one of them was forced to drop out by reason of death or sickness, another was chosen to take his place, so that they were never more nor less than ten thousand. They had the richest dress of any of the soldiers, with much gold on it, because they were the best men in the army. They had carriages with them and numbers of well-outfitted servants. Their food was brought to them on camels and baggage animals, separately from the rest of the army.

There were 1,207 triremes furnished by the Phoenicians, the Syrians, the Egyptians, the Cyprians, and many others, including the Greeks of Asia who were subject to the Persians, and the people of the islands. There were Persian fighting men on all the ships.

When the army had been counted and divided up

according to nations, Xerxes had all the troops drawn up in order and rode past them in a chariot. Then he had the ships drawn up in a line four hundred feet from the shore. They were anchored with their prows turned toward the land. When he had finished inspecting the army, Xerxes left his chariot and went on board a ship where he sat under a golden canopy. Then he reviewed the ships, sailing along between the prows and the land. The fighting men were all drawn up on the decks, in full battle dress.

After this Xerxes continued on his march toward Greece, forcing all the able-bodied men he found on the way to join his army. All the towns were compelled to feed the Persians as they passed by, and all kinds of delicacies which had to be served in gold and silver cups and bowls, were required for Xerxes. Everywhere the Persians passed, the Greeks were left behind, starving and penniless. The fleet sailed along the coast and passed through the canal at Athos.

THE PREDICTIONS
OF THE ORACLES

Not all the Greeks felt the same way about fighting the Persians. Some of them thought there were not enough warships in the whole of Greece to meet the invader. In fact, the great majority did not wish to become involved in the war, and were very ready to side with the Persians. It was true that the Athenians should be called the saviors of Greece, for they were the leaders, and whatever they did, many of the Greeks would follow their example.

The Athenians stood firm even when the oracles that came from Delphi were alarming. When the Athenians sent to ask what they should do, the first oracle advised them to flee their city. They were frightened by this, but did not wish to abandon Athens, and so they sent and requested a second oracle. This repeated the prediction that Athens itself would be lost, but spoke of a wooden wall provided by Zeus, and made a mysterious allusion to the island of Salamis, which lay off the coast of Attica, opposite Athens. The words of the oracle were in part very puzzling:

Pallas Athene, the goddess of Athens,
Cannot persuade great Zeus of Olympus
By prayer or by many words.
All shall be taken and lost in the borders of Athens.
Nevertheless Zeus will give the race of the Athenians
A wooden wall which shall not fail, and shall aid you
     and your children.
Do not wait for the warriors, on horse and on foot,
Who will come to you by land, but give way and turn
     your back.
Salamis, divine island! You will destroy the children
     of women
At the time when the wheat is planted or harvested.

When the oracles were brought back to Athens, people understood in different ways. Some of the older men thought that the god meant that the Acropolis would be saved; for in earlier times the Acropolis had been defended by a hedge of thorns, and they thought that this was what was meant by the "wooden wall." But others were convinced that the god, in speaking of a "wooden wall," meant their ships, and their advice was that all their efforts should be put into getting the ships ready for battle.

One of the leading men in Athens at this time was Themistocles, a man of good family who was noted for his public service. It was his opinion that the most important thing for the security of Athens was a strong navy, and he had already, before this time, been able to convince the people that he was right. This happened when some new silver mines, which were the public property of the city of Athens, were opened up at Laurium, in the eastern part of Attica. These mines turned out to be unexpectedly rich, and produced a much higher income than had been looked for. The people of Athens were about to divide up the profit among themselves. But Themistocles was able to persuade them to build two hundred new warships instead, and it was in this fashion that the ships later were ready to serve Greece in her time of need.

So when the second oracle came from Delphi, Themistocles interpreted it to mean that Athens would be saved by its navy. He convinced the people that this was what the god meant, and so the Athenians resolved to put their trust in heaven and meet the foreign invaders with all the power of their fleet.

The Greeks knew something of the power of the Persians, because of the spies that had been sent to Sardis while Xerxes was still there with his army. The spies reached Sardis, and learned the information they wanted about the king's army; but they were discovered, and after having been examined under torture by the Persian generals, they were taken away to be executed. So they were condemned to die; but when

Xerxes heard what had happened, he disapproved of the decision of his generals and ordered some of his bodyguards to bring the spies to him if they were found still alive. They found them alive and brought them before the king. He, then, when he learned why the spies had come, ordered his guards to take them around and show them his whole army, both horse and foot; and when the spies had seen everything they wished, he commanded his guards to send them away, wherever they wished to go.

When he had given this order, he explained it by pointing out that if the spies had been executed, the Greeks would not have had advance notice of his strength, and the Persians would not have done much harm to the enemy by putting three men to death. "But if these men return to Greece," he said, "when the Greeks hear of my power, even before the expedition sets out they will surrender this precious freedom of theirs, and there will be no reason for us to make an expedition against them."

So the spies returned to Greece and told what they had seen. Some of the cities in Greece determined to resist the invaders, while others were frightened by the rumors of the Persians' power and decided it would be safer to submit to the foreigners and cooperate with them. The people of Thessaly, the place the Persians would reach first, began by asserting they would defend themselves, and they persuaded some of the cities of

Greece to send them help; but when the Greeks came to Thessaly, the reports that reached them about the Persians made them so uneasy that they returned to Greece, and so the people of Thessaly found themselves unable to resist the Persians.

While this was happening, there was a council in progress at the Isthmus attended by the chosen representatives of all the Greek cities south of Thessaly that were still determined to resist the invaders. They believed that it would not be possible, with their small forces, to stop the Persians anywhere in the open plains of Thessaly. But Greece was a country of mountains; and there was one point, at the passage from Thessaly into Greece, that the Greeks thought they would be able to defend.

THE PASS AT
THERMOPYLAE

Thessaly and Greece were separated from each other by a long range of impassable mountains which ran right down to the Aegean Sea. There was a narrow strip of shore between the mountain and the sea, and the road from Thessaly to Greece ran along this strip of land. All along the west of the road rises a high mountain. To the east there was nothing but marshes and the sea.

At one point the mountain and the sea came so close together that the ground along the shore was only fifty feet wide. This place was called Thermopylae, the name—"Hot Gates" in Greek—having been given to it because there were springs of hot sulphurous water along the foot of the mountain in which people bathed because they thought the water had the power to heal diseases. The Greeks who lived south of the pass had built a wall at Thermopylae because they were afraid that the Thessalians might come and occupy their territory.

This was the place at which the Greeks, at their meeting at the Isthmus, thought they could resist the Persians successfully; for in this small space the enormous size of the Persian army would be of no advantage, and—what was very important to the Greeks—the Persians would not be able to use their cavalry at all. The Greeks were confident that, man for man, they were a match for the Persians; and so it was here that they could meet the invaders of their homeland.

AN ARMY OF FIVE MILLION

All this time the Persian army had been growing as the Persians forced the men they found on their march into their service. The Persians suffered no losses until they came to Thermopylae; and I made the following calculation of the size of the Persian host as it was at this time.

93

Since there were, as I have already said, 1,207 ships furnished by the people in Asia, and since there were about 200 men in each ship—170 rowers and 30 fighting men—the total in these ships was 241,400 men. In addition to the usual 30 fighters, each ship had on board 30 more fighting men, Persians or Medes or Sacae. This makes an additional total of 36,210 men in the ships.

To this I add the crews of the smaller ships, which had 50 oars; each of these crews was 80 men, more or less. There were 3,000 of these small ships, so they must have contained about 240,000 men. And so the total of men in all the ships which came from Asia was 517,610.

Of the land forces I calculated the infantry to be 1,700,100 and the cavalry to be 80,000. To these should be added the Arabians who fought on camels and the charioteers from Libya; I reckon these at 20,000.

Thus the total of the land and sea forces is 2,317,-710 men. This number represents the active forces that came from Asia and does not include the service units or the ships that brought food from Asia and their crews.

But to all this must be added the forces that came from Europe. Some of these had joined the Persians voluntarily; others had been forced into service.

The Greeks in Thrace and the islands off the coast

of Thrace had supplied 120 ships, and the rowers and fighting men in these must have totaled 24,000 men. The land forces furnished by all the different people that lived in Thrace I estimate at 300,000. Added to the numbers who came from Asia, this makes the total of all the fighting men 2,641,710.

As for the service units and the crews of the ships that carried provisions, I suppose that these can have been no fewer in number than the fighting men. If we assume that they were the same number, neither less nor more, then the total size of the forces of Xerxes was 5,283,420.

As for the cooks, who were women, and the other women who came with the army, there is no way of knowing how many of them there were. And no one knows the number of the pack animals and the Indian dogs that went with the army. So it is not surprising to me that people said that the streams ran dry when the Persian army passed; I am only astonished that there was food for so many people.

While the Persian army was marching through Thessaly toward Thermopylae, the fleet was sailing along the coast, trying to keep abreast of the army. Because it was sailing in strange waters, the fleet used to anchor off the shore every night. The ships which arrived first would anchor close to the land, the others outside of them.

THE STORM
OFF MAGNESIA

One night, as the fleet was sailing along the coast of
Magnesia, the anchorage was so small that the ships
had to be drawn up eight deep. The night was clear
and calm; but at dawn the sea began to churn and boil,
and there fell upon the ships a great storm and a high
wind from the east, which the people who lived in that
country call the Hellespont storm.

The Persians who saw that the wind was rising, and
were anchored in a position in which they could do
this, dragged their ships up on the beach before the
storm broke, and so they and their ships survived; but
the ships that the storm caught at anchor were partly
driven on rocks and partly on the beach. Some were
driven some distance and wrecked. Indeed it was a
storm that was very difficult to survive.

In that disaster there perished, at the lowest estimate, at least four hundred ships. The losses of men
could not be counted, and an enormous amount of

valuable equipment was lost. One of the Greeks who lived in that neighborhood collected many gold and silver drinking cups that were cast up on the beach, and a great deal of Persian treasure. Thanks to his good luck he became very rich; but he was not happy in all respects, for he had the misfortune to kill his own son accidentally.

The merchant vessels which carried food, and the other ships that were destroyed, could not even be counted. The admirals of the fleet were afraid that the Thessalians would attack them while they were in difficulties, and to protect themselves, they built a high barricade on the beach out of the wreckage.

The storm lasted for three days and abated on the fourth. Greek lookouts had been watching from the heights of the island of Euboea and on the second day of the storm they ran down and told the commanders of the Greek fleet, which was anchored near by, about the Persians' losses. On this the Greeks offered prayer and libation to Poseidon for having delivered them.

Xerxes and his army continued their march and camped about five miles from Thermopylae. The Greeks camped in the pass, halfway between the two entrances.

THE ADVANCE GUARD AT THERMOPYLAE

The following Greek forces were waiting for the Persians at Thermopylae:

```
 300 from Sparta
 500 from Tegea
 500 from Mantinea
 120 from Orchomenus in Arcadia
1000 from the rest of Arcadia
 400 from Corinth
 200 from Phlius
  80 from Mycenae
 700 from Thespiae
 400 from Thebes
─────
4200
```

Besides these, there were all the available men of eastern Locris, and one thousand men from Phocis. The Greeks who had already arrived at Thermopylae had sent messengers to summon the Locrians and the

Phocians, who had not originally joined with them. The messengers told the Locrians and the Phocians that the Greeks at Thermopylae were an advance guard; that the rest of the allies were expected every day; that the sea was well guarded by the Athenians and the people of Aegina and all the rest who had joined to make up the naval force. There was nothing, the messengers said, that they had to fear; it was not a god that was invading Greece, but a man; there was no mortal man to whom, at his birth, there was not allotted some misfortune; and to the greatest of men the greatest of misfortunes occurred. Therefore it was sure that the man who was coming against them, being only a mortal, would fail to gain what he expected. When they heard this, the Locrians and the Phocians set out to help the Greeks at Thermopylae.

The force from each city had its own general; but the one who was most respected and was the leader of the whole army was Leonidas the Spartan. His descent was traced back to Herakles and he was king of Sparta. He had never expected to be king, for he had two older brothers; but they both died without leaving sons, and the office came to Leonidas.

The Spartans sent these three hundred men with Leonidas in advance of the rest of their force, so that when the rest of the allies saw them they might join the war themselves and not go over to the Persians. This might happen if they knew that the Spartans were postponing their own entry into the war. The Spartans sent only an advance guard because they were waiting for the feast of the Carnea, the national festival in honor of Apollo, which was celebrated in September. Their religious beliefs prevented them from setting out on a campaign before they celebrated this festival. But when they had kept the feast, they intended to leave a garrison at Sparta and set out with their whole military force and march at top speed.

The rest of the allies planned to do similar things themselves. An Olympic festival was due to be celebrated at about the same time and so they sent only their advance guards, not expecting that the war at Thermopylae would be decided so quickly.

THE PERSIANS ARRIVE

This was what they intended. But when they saw the Persians coming near the entrance to the pass, the Greeks in Thermopylae began to be fearful and debated whether to leave or to stay. All the men from the Peloponnese except the Spartans were in favor of returning to the Peloponnese and guarding the Isthmus. The Phocians and the Locrians, who would not have the protection of the Isthmus, were highly indignant at this idea, and Leonidas voted for remaining where they were and sending messengers to the cities to demand help, seeing that they themselves at Thermopylae were too few to drive away the Persians.

While they were debating, Xerxes sent a mounted scout to see how many they were and what they were doing. While he was still in Thessaly he had heard that a small army was being collected here; and he had heard that its leaders were Spartans and that their commander was Leonidas, a descendant of Herakles.

The scout rode up to the camp and looked it over, though he did not see the whole of it. He would not have been able to see those who were stationed on the other side of the wall, which they had rebuilt and were guarding. He did, however, learn about those who were on the outside of the wall, and it happened that at that time the Spartans were taking their turn to be on guard there. He saw some of them exercising stripped and others combing their hair. He was astonished at the sight and made a note of their number. When he had learned everything he could, he rode back at leisure; no one pursued him or indeed paid any attention to him. So he went back and told Xerxes about everything he had seen.

When Xerxes heard this he was unable to understand what the truth was—namely, that the Spartans were getting ready to kill to the best of their power or to be killed. What they were doing seemed to him laughable, and he sent for Demaratus, the former king of Sparta, who had come with the army. The Spartan constitution provided for two kings at once, there being two so that, if necessary, each could act as a check on the other. Demaratus had opposed his colleague Cleomenes (Leonidas' older brother) so much that Cleomenes arranged to have Demaratus dethroned. Demaratus then fled to the court of King Darius, and later accompanied Xerxes, hoping that the Persians, when they were victorious, would restore him to his office.

When Demaratus arrived, Xerxes questioned him about all these things, hoping to learn what it was that the Spartans were doing.

Demaratus answered, "You have heard from me before about these men, when we were starting out against Greece; but when you heard what I said you laughed at me, though I told you of what I saw clearly would be the outcome of these things. My greatest desire is to speak the truth in your presence, O King. Now please hear me again: These men have come to do battle with us for this pass, and that is what they are preparing for. It is their custom to arrange their hair carefully when they are about to risk their lives. You may be sure of this, that if you conquer these men and those who remain behind in Sparta, there is no other nation of mankind, O King, that will be able to withstand you when you come upon them. You are now face to face with the finest royalty and the noblest city and the bravest men in Greece."

But it seemed to Xerxes that what Demaratus said was altogether incredible, and he questioned him further, asking in what fashion these men would fight against his army when they were so few.

"O King," Demaratus replied, "treat me as you would a liar, if these things do not turn out as I say."

THE PERSIANS
ATTACK
THE PASS

In spite of this, he did not convince Xerxes. The king waited for four days, always supposing that the Greeks would flee. But on the fifth day, since they did not leave, it seemed to him that they were shameless and foolish to remain; and he became angry and sent the Medes and the Cissians against them, commanding them to take the Greeks alive and bring them to him.

The Medes came upon the Greeks at top speed and fell upon them. Many of the Medes were killed, but others came to the attack after them, and though they had severe losses they were not driven off. But they made it clear to everyone, and not least to the king himself, that although there were many of them, in terms of human beings, there were few real men among them. This fight lasted the whole day.

When the Medes received such rough treatment, they withdrew, and the Persians, whom the king called The Immortals, took their place and attacked, led by Hydarnes. It was thought that they would finish off the Greeks with ease; but when they came hand to hand with the Greeks, they had no greater success than the Medes, but had just the same experience, for they were fighting in a narrow space and were using shorter spears than the Greeks, so that they were not able to gain any advantage from their greater numbers.

The Spartans all this time fought in a manner worthy of praise. They showed that they were skilled soldiers fighting against unskilled troops. One of their devices was to turn their backs and pretend to flee; and when the barbarians saw them apparently fleeing, they would rush after them with a great deal of noise and shouting. But when the Spartans were about to be caught, they would turn and strike down innumerable Persians; and a few of the Spartans themselves were killed as well. So when the Persians were not able to gain the entrance to the pass in any way, though they attacked both by companies and in every other fashion, they withdrew.

While these attacks were going on, the king was watching from his throne, and it is reported that he sprang up three times out of fear for his army.

This was the outcome of the fighting on the first day, and on the following day the barbarians performed no better. They attacked again, supposing that the Greeks were so few that by this time they were disabled and would not be able to resist. But the Greeks were drawn up by formations and by nations, and in this way they all fought in turn, except for the Phocians, who were stationed on the mountain to guard the path which led round the pass on the top of the mountain. So when the Persians found that nothing was different from the day before, they retired.

THE TRAITOR REVEALS THE PATH OVER THE MOUNTAIN

The king was at a loss as to how to deal with the situation, and while he was wondering what to do, a man came into his presence named Epialtes, from Malis. Hoping to obtain a large reward from the king, he told him of the path which led over the top of the mountain to Thermopylae. By doing this, he destroyed the Greeks who had been left there. Later he fled to Thessaly, for fear of the Spartans; a price was put on his head and he was finally killed.

This was the fate of Epialtes at a later time. Xerxes was pleased with what Epialtes proposed to do, and gladly sent Hydarnes and the men under his command.

They started out from the camp at about the time when the lamps are lit.

This path had been discovered by the people of Malis at the time when the Phocians built a wall across the pass at Thermopylae. The path made it possible to cross the mountains without using the pass the Spartans and the other Greeks were defending; it began on the Persian side of Thermopylae, near Xerxes' camp, and led to a point on the other side of Thermopylae, to the rear of the Greeks.

The Persians marched all night and at sunrise came to the highest point of the mountain. In this part of the mountain, as I said, a thousand Phocians were on guard, both defending their own country and guarding the path. This was in accordance with the promise they had voluntarily given to Leonidas.

The barbarians escaped notice as they came up the mountain, because it was covered with oak trees. The Phocians finally learned of their coming because the weather was calm and quiet, and the barbarians made a good bit of noise as they made their way through the oak leaves which were strewn on the ground.

When the Phocians noticed the Persians, they sprang up and put on their armor, and all at once the barbarians were upon them. When they saw men putting on armor, the Persians were astonished, for they had expected that no one would appear against them and here they came upon an army.

Hydarnes was afraid these men might be Spartans and asked Epialtes what part of Greece they came from. When he learned who they were he drew up the Persians in battle formation. The Phocians then found themselves under a steady and heavy fire of arrows; and supposing that the Persians' only purpose was to attack them, they retreated and fled to the top of the mountain and prepared to fight to the death. But the Persians with Epialtes and Hydarnes paid no attention to the Phocians and started down the mountain as fast as they could go.

The Greeks at Thermopylae first had warning of the death that was coming to them with the dawn from the seer Megistias when he examined the daily offerings according to custom and saw what they foretold. Soon there came deserters from the Persian army, who told them of the barbarians coming over the mountain. These came while it was still night. Finally the lookouts came running down from the top of the mountain when day was beginning to dawn.

Immediately the Greeks held a council. Their opinions were divided, some not wishing to leave their post, while others thought the opposite. After a time they broke up into two groups and some left and returned, each to his home, while the others prepared to remain where they were with Leonidas.

There is a report that Leonidas himself ordered some of the men to leave because he was responsible for them and did not wish to have them lose their lives, though he thought it was not proper for himself and the Spartans who were with him to leave the post they had come to defend. But I myself am rather more inclined toward the other explanation—namely, that when Leonidas saw that the allies were fainthearted and did not wish to face every risk with him, he commanded them to leave, though it was not right for himself to go. If he remained, he would leave behind him great fame and the prosperity of Sparta would not be destroyed. For when the Spartans consulted the oracle concerning the war, when it was first beginning, the Pythian priestess had given them the following prophecy: Either Sparta would be destroyed by the barbarians or its king would be killed. It was of this, I believe, that Leonidas was thinking, and it was for this reason, I think, that he sent the allies away, so that the Spartans should have all the glory.

THE
LAST
FIGHT

Xerxes offered libations at sunrise, according to custom. He then waited until the middle of the morning and made his attack. This was on the advice of the traitor Epialtes. The path down from the mountain is much shorter than the way the Persians had to take to reach the top; and so the Persians, leaving the top of the pass at dawn, would reach the low ground and the pass at about the middle of the morning.

So when Xerxes' barbarians attacked, the Greeks with Leonidas, knowing that they were setting out to their death, advanced much farther than they had been accustomed to do, and went into the wide part of the pass. Before this they had concentrated on guarding the wall of the pass, and on all the earlier days of the fighting they had drawn together into the narrow part of the pass and had fought there. Now they met the enemy outside of the narrow part, and many of the foreigners fell there. There were many killed because their officers came behind them with whips in their hands and lashed the men to force them to go forward.

Many of the foreigners fell into the sea and were drowned, and even more were knocked down and trampled to death by their comrades, for no one paid any attention to who it was who was perishing. The Greeks knew that death was coming to them from the foreigners who were making their way round to their rear over the mountain, and so they put forth all their strength against the foreigners and fought desperately and recklessly.

In time, most of them had broken their spears, and they were slaying the Persians with their swords. In that heavy fighting Leonidas fell, having shown himself to be the bravest of men. With him there fell other famous Spartans whose names I learned because of their great valor, as I also learned the names of all the three hundred. Many distinguished Persians were killed as well.

Two brothers of Xerxes were killed in the fighting, and there was a great contest between the Persians and the Spartans over the body of Leonidas, until the Greeks, through their bravery, dragged it out of the fight and drove the enemy away from it four times.

This fighting continued until the men with the traitor Epialtes arrived. When the Greeks realized that they had come, the battle became something different. The Greeks now withdrew to the narrow part of the road and passed behind the wall, and all—except the

Thebans—stationed themselves on the little hill in the entrance to the pass, where a stone statue of a lion has now been set up in honor of Leonidas (whose name means "little lion").

Here they defended themselves with their swords, as long as they had them, and then with fists and teeth, until the foreigners overwhelmed them and struck them down. Some foreigners attacked them from the front, climbing over the ruins of the wall, and others came from behind, all taking their stand around them in a ring.

Such was the bravery of the Spartans. Yet the bravest of them all, it is said, was the Spartan Dieneces. A saying of his was reported before they joined battle with the Medes. Someone told him that the foreigners were so numerous that when they discharged their bows, the sun was hidden by the dense throng of arrows. Dieneces was not at all frightened by these words, but made a joke of the number of Medes and replied to his friend that if the Medes hid the sun with their arrows, then the Greeks would fight in the shade and not in the sun.

THE GRAVES OF
THE HEROES

The men who fell in this last fight, and those who had been killed before Leonidas sent the allies away, were all buried where they fell, and there is an inscription, as follows:

Four thousand here from the land of Pelops
Once made a stand against three million.

This was the inscription for all of the dead together. There was a special one for the Spartans:

O Stranger, go tell the Spartans
That we obeyed their orders, and now lie here.

That is for the Spartans; and the following epitaph is for the seer:

This is the tomb of the famous Megistias,
Whom the Medes slew.
A seer, he knew well the fate that was coming.
But did not choose to leave the Spartan warriors.

113

THE FATE OF
THE THEBANS

The Thebans, whose general was Leontiades, found themselves compelled to fight against the king's army so long as they were with the Greeks. But when they saw that the Persians were winning, and that Leonidas and his men were pressing toward the little hill, the Thebans separated from them and went toward the foreigners, holding out their hands and calling out that they were on the side of the Medes and that they had been the first to offer earth and water to the king as a sign of submission. They said that it was under compulsion that they had come to Thermopylae and that they bore no guilt for the harm done to the king.

All this was one of the truest things ever spoken and, by saying it, they saved themselves, and the Thessalians, who had already joined the Persians, were there as witnesses to what they said. However, they were not wholly successful, for when the foreigners first found them coming upon them, they killed some of them when they came close. Most of them, by Xerxes' command, were branded with the royal brand, beginning with the general Leontiades.

XERXES AFTER THE BATTLE

After the fighting was over, Xerxes sent for Demaratus, the former Spartan king, who was with him, and asked how many Spartans were left, and whether they were all warriors like these. When Demaratus answered that there were many of them, the king inquired as to what he thought would be the best way to conquer them.

Demaratus' advice was that the king send three hundred of his ships to take up stations off the coast of Sparta. With this force of the Persians so near them, the Spartans would never leave their country to help the other Greeks; and the Persians would then be able to move against the rest of the Greeks and defeat them.

But one of Xerxes' brothers, who was admiral of the fleet, was opposed to this plan. He reminded the king that he had recently lost four hundred of his ships in a storm, and that if he now sent away three hundred more, he would make what remained of his fleet so weak that it would be defeated easily. The admiral advised keeping the fleet and the army together.

Xerxes preferred his brother's advice, though he made it plain that he did not intend any slight to Demaratus. The king then visited the battlefield and walked among the corpses; and when he heard about Leonidas and how he had been king and general of the Spartans, he ordered his men to cut off Leonidas' head and impale it on a pole. It is plain to me from this and from many other signs that Xerxes had been much more hostile to Leonidas than to the others. Otherwise he would not have treated his body in such an inhuman way, for the Persians, of all the people I know, are the most ready to honor men for bravery in war. So Xerxes' men carried out their orders.

THE SEA BATTLE
AT ARTEMISIUM

During the very same days as the fighting at Thermopylae, the Persian fleet and the Greek fleet were meeting each other off Cape Artemisium, on the northern shore of Euboea. It was here that the Greek ships had collected, hoping to stop the advance of the Persian navy.

The Greeks at Artemisium had 271 warships, plus nine fifty-oared galleys. The chief admiral was the Spartan, Eurybiades, for the allies had declared that they would rather have Eurybiades in command than any of the Athenians, and that if the Athenians were in command they would leave. The Athenians accepted this because they thought a united defense was the most important thing, and they would give up the leadership which naturally belonged to them for the sake of harmony.

But when the Greeks heard that the Persian fleet was approaching, and had word of its size and strength, they lost their courage and were all for turning and going home. There were some, however, who wanted to stay. These were unable to persuade Eurybiades to keep the fleet at Artemisium, but when he could not be moved, they went to Themistocles, the admiral of the Athenian ships. He was able to convince Eurybiades, and, along with him, some of the other commanders; and so it was that the Greek fleet stayed at Artemisium.

The Persians, as they sailed down the coast, first sighted the Greeks near the island of Sciathus in the early part of the afternoon. But the Persians did not plan a frontal attack, for they were afraid that the Greeks would take to flight and that they would escape under cover of the night; and this would defeat the Persians' purpose, for they wanted to destroy the Greeks, not drive them away.

So the Persians adopted the following plan: They sent two hundred of their ships to sail round the other side of the island of Sciathus and continue all the way round Euboea so as to come down on the Greeks from the rear while the main Persian fleet attacked them from the front. The Persians made no attack on the Greeks that day; they would have to wait for the signal that would tell them that the ships sailing round to the rear of the Greeks were ready.

There was a Greek with the Persian fleet, the best diver of his time, who had saved much treasure for the Persians when their ships had been wrecked and had also gained much for himself at the same time. This man had long intended to desert the Persians and join the Greeks, but he had never had an opportunity. He now was able to escape in a small boat, and he came to Artemisium and told the Greek admirals about the ships that were sailing round Euboea to take them in the rear.

The Greeks at first decided to wait until after midnight and then set out to meet the ships that were sailing round. But when they saw that the Persians were not going to attack them, they waited for the late afternoon and set sail against the foreigners.

When Xerxes' commanders saw the Greeks sailing at them with so few ships, they thought they were certainly mad, and they set out with their own ships, expecting to win easily, as was very natural since the Greek ships were so few and their own were so much more numerous and also more seaworthy.

With all this confidence, the Persians surrounded the Greek ships, and each Persian commander was eager to be the first to capture an Athenian ship and receive a reward from the king, for the Athenians were the most talked about in the fleet.

The Greeks were ready for this, and at a signal they all drew the sterns of their ships together, so that the prows faced the foreigners. Then, when the second signal was given, they all set to work, although they were confined in a narrow space and were fighting prow to prow.

In the end the Greeks had captured thirty of the foreigners' ships. The outcome of this fighting was doubtful, and night put an end to the battle. The Greeks returned to Artemisium and the Persians went back to their original position, having accomplished far less than they had hoped.

It was the middle of the summer; and when night came on, it began to rain hard. There was heavy rain all night, with violent thunder from the mountains. The corpses and the wreckage were driven by the wind and the current toward the Persian ships as they lay at anchor, and the bodies and the timbers and ropes became entangled with the prows of the Persian ships and with the oars. The crews and the fighting men were alarmed; they thought they were going to be destroyed, after having gone through the shipwreck and the storm that had already done so much damage.

The night was much more cruel to the ships that were sailing round Euboea, for the storm and the rain came upon them when they were in the open sea. The ships were driven out of control, and no one on board knew where they were going. Finally they were driven on the rocks and the ships broke up. This was all done by the providence of heaven, so that the Persian force should be made equal to that of the Greeks and should no longer be superior to it.

When day came, the main part of the Persian fleet stayed where it was, for the Persians were in such a poor state that they were satisfied not to make any move for the present. During the morning, fifty-three Athenian ships arrived to help the Greeks. The Greeks were cheered both by the arrival of the ships and by the news that the foreign ships which were sailing round Euboea had all been lost in the storm.

The Greeks waited for the late afternoon, as they had done the day before, and then set sail against the Persians. They destroyed some ships and when it was dark sailed back to Artemisium.

The Persian admirals were now afraid of Xerxes' anger, and they took it very badly that so few ships should do them so much damage; and on the third day they did not wait for the Greeks to start the fight but issued the orders and set sail about noon.

The Greeks waited calmly at their station off Artemisium. The Persians formed a half-moon with their ships and attempted to encircle the Greeks.

When they saw the Persians' plan, the Greeks made a charge and met the foreigners. In this fight each side had about equal success. Xerxes' force did itself harm because of the size of the fleet and the crowd of the ships, for the vessels got into confusion and ran into each other. However, they held out and would not surrender, for they were ashamed to be put to flight by such a small number of ships. Many Greeks ships and many of their fighting men perished, but many more of the foreigners' ships and men were lost.

So they fought in this way until they drew apart and sailed away, glad to return to their anchorages. The Greeks had possession of the wrecks and the bodies, but they had been roughly treated—especially the Athenians, half of whose ships had been damaged.

THE PERSIANS ADVANCE ON ATHENS

The sea fight took place on the same days as the fight at Thermopylae. It had been arranged beforehand that a messenger with a small boat was to be ready at Artemisium to take the news of the sea battle, if there was one, to Thermopylae, while another messenger, with a thirty-oared galley, was stationed at Thermopylae, ready to take the news to the fleet if any misfortune came to the land army. So when the news came to the fleet of the death of Leonidas and his men, the admirals decided to sail for the waters of Attica where they could protect Athens, for they knew there was now no force that could stop the Persians, and everyone expected that the foreigners would make Athens their next goal.

FROM THERMOPYLAE TO SALAMIS

When the fighting at Thermopylae had opened up the land route into Greece, Xerxes was eager to conquer Athens as soon as possible; but he was also very anxious to make his own people think that their losses at Thermopylae had not been as great as they were. Twenty thousand Persians had been killed, and four thousand Greeks. So Xerxes left about a thousand of the Persian corpses lying on the ground and buried the rest in trenches which were filled in and covered with leaves. Then he brought together in one place all the four thousand Greek bodies. When he had arranged all this, Xerxes invited all the members of the fleet to come and visit the battlefield. They all came eagerly and spent a day viewing the bodies, though nobody was really deceived by the difference between the Persian dead and the Greek dead.

The next day the Persian army set out on its march. In some of the territory the foreigners passed through, the Greeks joined them out of fear; but in other places, when the Greeks did not come over to their side, the Persians burned the towns and villages and temples, and ruined the crops in the fields.

All this time the people of Athens knew that the Persian army was advancing on them. When the Greek fleet left Artemisium, the Athenians begged the ships to anchor at the island of Salamis, which lay off the coast of Attica. This was because they hoped to send the women and children out of Athens to Salamis, where they would be safer. An official proclamation was made at Athens that every man in the city must be responsible for saving his children and his servants and slaves.

Ships from other cities now came to Salamis, so that the fleet that gathered there was even larger than it had been at Artemisium. Altogether there were 378 warships, plus a number of fifty-oared galleys. The Athenians, as was fitting to their position as the leading sea power among the Greeks, furnished more ships than any other single city, namely 180. Eurybiades the Spartan was chief admiral.

When all the ships were collected at Salamis, the captains held a council to decide where it would be best for them to meet the Persian fleet. There were various opinions; but while they were still debating, a messenger from Athens came to say that the foreigners had reached Attica and were burning the whole countryside.

It had taken the Persians a month to pass from Asia into Europe and another three months to reach Athens. When they entered the city they found it deserted; but later they discovered that some Greeks had stayed behind in the temple of Athena on the Acropolis. These were the custodians of the temple, plus some men who were so poor that they had nothing to save by moving to Salamis.

When they reached the Acropolis, the Persians found that these men had barricaded the place with doors and logs. The Persians then occupied the Areopagus, the "hill of Ares," which is opposite the Acropolis, and began the siege in this way. They wrapped arrows in burning tow and shot them against the barricade. While they were doing this, they sent men to try to force an entrance.

The men on the Acropolis defended themselves by rolling stones down on the foreigners. After a long time the Persians still could not capture the Acropolis and Xerxes was at a loss as to what to do.

Finally some of the foreigners found a means of

entrance. On the front of the Acropolis, behind the public way that led up to the gates, there was a steep cleft in the rock, so steep that it was not guarded, for no one supposed that it would be possible to climb up that way. Some Persian soldiers found the cleft and managed to reach the top; and when the Athenians saw that the Persians had made their way to the top of the Acropolis, some of them threw themselves down from the wall and perished, and others took refuge in the inner chamber of the temple. The Persian soldiers who had been the first to get to the top of the Acropolis immediately went to the gates and opened them and then killed the men who had sought safety in the temple; and when they had killed everyone on the Acropolis, they plundered the temple of Athena and burned everything on the Acropolis.

When the word came to the Greeks in Salamis of what had happened at the Athenian Acropolis, it put them into such an uproar that some of the commanders would not wait for the outcome of the debate on where they were to meet the Persian fleet, but hurried aboard their own ships and ran up their sails for instant flight. The commanders who remained behind decided that the fleet should fight at the Isthmus of Corinth, where there was the narrow land passage between mainland Greece and the Peloponnese. When night came they left the meeting and embarked on their own ships.

When Themistocles returned to his own ship after

the council, one of the men on board asked him what had been decided. When this man learned that it had been decided to sail to the Isthmus and to defend the Peloponnese, he pointed out to Themistocles that if the ships left Salamis, they would all go back to their own cities, not to the Isthmus. Neither Eurybiades nor anyone else would be able to keep them in hand, and Greece would perish by this foolishness.

Themistocles was impressed by what his friend said. He returned to Eurybiades' ship and told him that he wished to speak with him on a matter of the public interest. Eurybiades invited him to come on board and say whatever he wished; so Themistocles sat down beside him and told him of his friend's views and added many other arguments of his own. Finally he was able to persuade the Spartan to leave his ship and collect the admirals in the place where they held their meetings.

When the commanders had been brought together, before Eurybiades spoke on the reason for calling the meeting, Themistocles took the lead and spoke as strongly as he could. He pointed out that if they fought at the Isthmus, they would be fighting in open waters which would be to their disadvantage since their ships were heavier than the Persians' and fewer in number; whereas if they stayed at Salamis and fought, they would have the advantage of being in a smaller bay, so that the Persian ships, by reason of their great number, would interfere with each other. And of course they would save Salamis where the Athenian women and children had been taken. By fighting at Salamis, they would in fact be defending the Isthmus.

When Themistocles had finished, there was a long and bitter argument, for the commanders from the other cities were jealous of Athens, and they were thinking more of their own cities than of Greece. But Themistocles answered very warmly, pointing out that the Athenians had two hundred ships, fully outfitted and with their complete forces of sailors and fighting men; and this made Athens the strongest single power in Greece.

For a final argument, Themistocles declared that if the rest of the Greeks did not stay at Salamis and fight, the Athenians would embark their households and sail to the town of Siris in southern Italy, which they had owned for a long time, and settle there; and the rest of the Greeks, without the strength of Athens, would perish.

In the end, Eurybiades decided that the whole fleet should remain at Salamis. In my opinion he did this because he was afraid that the Athenians would leave if he took the fleet to the Isthmus.

So the Greeks prepared for the sea battle where they were. At sunrise the next day there was an earthquake, both on land and at sea, and the Greeks offered prayers to all the gods.

THE PERSIANS
PREPARE
FOR BATTLE

When the men of the Persian fleet had gazed upon what had been done to the Spartans at Thermopylae, they waited three days and then set sail; and after three more days they came to the bay of Phalerum, near Athens. So far as I can tell, the Persian forces, both on land and at sea, were no smaller when they broke into Athens than they were when they came to Thermopylae and to Artemisium. The losses in the great storm and at Thermopylae and at Artemisium were made up by Greeks who joined Xerxes and followed him as he advanced deeper into Greece.

So when all this army had come to Athens, and the fleet to Phalerum, Xerxes came down from Athens to the fleet to visit the naval commanders and hear their opinions. When he had arrived and had taken his seat on his throne, there came into his presence the rulers of the various cities and the commanders from the ships, and they took seats according to the grades of honor that the king had granted them. First came the king of Sidon, then the king of Tyre, and then all the rest. When they had sat down in order, one after the other, Xerxes sent Mardonius, the Persian general who was the nephew of Darius, to test the wisdom of each man by asking him whether the Persians should engage in a naval battle.

When Mardonius went around putting the question to them, beginning with the king of Sidon, all together uttered the same opinion, namely to give battle at sea —all, that is, except for Artemisia, the queen of Halicarnassus in Asia, who had served with distinction as commander of the men of Halicarnassus and of the five ships that Halicarnassus furnished.

It was a remarkable thing that a woman should follow Xerxes, along with the other commanders. She was the widow of the king of Halicarnassus; but she did not need to come with the Persians as the commander of her people, for she had a grown son. But she was fit for command and showed courage and good sense.

Artemisia spoke to Mardonius thus: "Tell the king, if you please, Mardonius, that I who say this am one who was not the last in courage in the fighting at Artemisium, and I am not one who accomplished the least at that time. My lord, it is right for me to make known my view, because I happen to think that it is what is best for your cause. Spare your ships, and do not fight at sea. It has been proved that the Greeks are better fighters at sea than the Persians. Why must you put yourself in danger by fighting a naval battle? Are you not in possession of Athens, which was one of the main objects of your expedition? Do you not control all of that part of Greece you have passed through?

"Let me say how I think it will go with your enemies. If you do not hurry to fight at sea, but hold your ships here, near the land, or even if you move on to the Peloponnese, you will easily gain everything you have come for. The Greeks will not be able to hold out against you for any length of time, but you will make them scatter and they will all flee, each to his city. They have no food with them in this island, I am told; and if you take your army into the Peloponnese, it is not likely that the men who have come from there will be content to remain here. They will have no interest in fighting sea battles for Athens. But if you hurry now to fight at sea, I fear that your fleet may be harmed and that this will bring harm to your army."

Artemisia's friends were sorry to hear her say this, for they thought the king would punish her in some way for advising against a battle at sea. But there were people who were jealous of Artemisia and wished her ill because of the place of honor she held among the allies; and these were pleased by her answer, for they thought it would lead to her destruction. But when the opinions of the commanders were reported to Xerxes, he was greatly pleased by Artemisia's opinion, for he had always thought that she was a woman of ability and now he held her in even higher regard. However, he gave orders that they should follow the opinion of the majority. What he had in mind was that at Artemisium his men had lacked spirit, since he was not present to watch them, but this time he intended to watch the battle himself.

THE NIGHT BEFORE THE BATTLE OF SALAMIS

The command to sail was given, and they put out for Salamis and took their places in order, at their convenience, without any opposition from the Greeks. There was not time enough left that day to begin the battle, for night came upon them, and so they made their preparations for the next day.

But among the Greeks there was acute fear, especially among those who came from the Peloponnese. Their fear came from the thought that they were in Salamis, about to fight for the land of the Athenians; and if they were beaten, they would be shut up and besieged in the island and would thereby be leaving their own land unprotected. On that very night the Persian army was on its way to the Peloponnese.

When the Greek commanders were holding their customary council, Themistocles found he was being outvoted by the Peloponnesians; so he secretly left the council and sent a man in a small boat to the Persian fleet, giving him a message that he must deliver. This man's name was Sicinnus; he was a slave of Themistocles, a member of the household who served as the attendant of Themistocles' sons when they were away from the house and at school. Later Themistocles gave him his freedom and made him a wealthy man.

Sicinnus arrived in his boat and was taken before the Persian admirals. This was what Themistocles had ordered him to say: "The admiral of the Athenians sent me secretly; the other Greeks know nothing about it. He is in sympathy with your king's purpose and he desires that your undertakings be successful, not the affairs of the Greeks. The admiral sent me to tell you that the Greeks have lost courage and are planning to flee. Now is the time that offers you the chance to carry out the best of all victories, if you do not allow the Greeks to escape. They cannot reach any agreement with each other, and they will not make a stand against you. You will see them fighting with each other—those who are your friends and those who are not."

When he had said this, he left as quickly as possible. The Persians believed the message; and during the night they first put ashore a large number of their men on the little island of Psyttalea, which lies between Salamis and the mainland. Then, at midnight, they moved their ships so that the Greeks at Salamis would be encircled on all sides and unable to escape by putting out to sea. In this way the Greeks would be punished for their successes off Artemisium.

The reason why the Persians put some of their men ashore at Psyttalea was this: that in a sea battle it was at this point especially that wrecked ships and men who had been thrown into the sea would be carried ashore—the island in fact lay directly in the path of the battle that was about to take place—and by having men on the island they would be able to save their own people and kill their enemies. All of this they carried out in silence, lest their enemies learn what was going on. They worked at this all night, without taking any rest.

As for the admirals in Salamis, there was much talk and argument; and they did not yet know that the foreigners had surrounded them with their ships, but supposed that they were still in the positions in which they had seen them drawn up during the day.

While they were arguing, there came over to Salamis in the dark Aristides, an Athenian, who had been a political enemy of Themistocles and had been exiled, though I am sure that he was one of the best and most

134

honest men in Athens. He came to the place where the meeting was being held and caused Themistocles to be called out of the meeting, though Themistocles was no friend of his but his worst enemy; but in the instant danger of the moment he put all that out of his mind and called Themistocles out of the council so that he might confer with him.

Aristides had already heard that the Peloponnesians were eager to sail to the Isthmus. So, as Themistocles came out to meet him, he said to him: "There has been rivalry between us before now as to which of us should do more good to our fatherland. Let it be the same now. I have come to tell you that it makes no difference whether the Peloponnesians talk much or little about sailing away from this place. For I have seen with my own eyes that which I tell you now. Not even if the Corinthians and Eurybiades himself wish to sail out of Salamis can they do so, for we are surrounded on every side by our enemies. Go into the meeting and tell them this."

"What you urge us to do is very useful," Themistocles answered. "Your news is good; you have seen yourself that which I was hoping would happen. Let me tell you that what the Persians are doing is of my own planning—for when the Greeks would not willingly prepare to fight, it was necessary to force them into it, even against their will.

"But since you have come bringing good news, tell

it to them yourself. If I tell it to them, they will think it is something I have invented, and I shall not be able to persuade them that the foreigners are doing as you say. But go yourself and tell them how things are. When you have spoken to them, if they trust you, that will be best. But if what you say does not convince them, it will be the same so far as we are concerned; for if we are encircled on every side, as you say, they will not be able to escape."

Aristides went into the council and told them what he had seen, and how hard it had been for him to pass through the Persian blockade. When he had spoken, he left, and the commanders began to argue again, for most of them did not believe the news that Aristides had brought.

While they were still unable to believe what they had heard, a warship came with some deserters, Greeks who had been forced to follow Xerxes and now found an opportunity to escape. They brought the same news, and this time the Greeks believed it. With another Greek ship which had deserted the Persians at Artemisium, this brought the Greek navy to 380 ships.

THE BATTLE

Now that the Greeks believed the reports about the Persians' position, they made their preparations for the battle. By this time it was the first light of dawn. A meeting of all the fighting men was called and Themistocles made a stirring speech which appealed to all the courage the men possessed. Then they were all sent back to their ships.

The Greeks set sail with all their vessels, and the foreigners at once came down upon them. The Greeks began to back water and run their ships on the beach—all, that is, save one Athenian ship, which pressed forward and engaged a Persian ship. The two vessels became entangled and could not be separated, and the other Greek ships came to the help of the first Athenian ship, and so the battle began.

The Greeks fought in orderly fashion and kept in formation; but the foreigners fell into disorder and followed no plan, so that it was natural that they should come to the end that they did. But on this day they fought much better than they had at Artemisium. Every man worked hard and feared Xerxes, each thinking that the king was looking at him.

There were many stories of what happened that day, and I cannot tell all of them accurately. But what happened to Artemisia gave her an even greater reputation with the king than she had had before. Xerxes' force by now was in great confusion and at this point Artemisia's ship was being pursued by an Athenian ship. The queen could not escape because there were Persian ships in her way and she was the closest of them to the enemy; and so she decided on something which later was much to her advantage. Still pursued by the Athenian warship, she charged at a friendly ship, from Calydna, one of the Greek cities on the coast of Asia which was subject to the Persian king. Whether she did this deliberately, because she had a quarrel with the king of that city, or whether the ship happened to get in her way, I cannot say. But she charged it and sank it, and thus won for herself two rewards. When the captain of the Athenian ship saw her charge and sink a ship of the foreigners, he supposed that Artemisia's ship either was a ship of the Greek fleet or a deserter from the foreigners, fighting against them, and so he turned away and looked for others to deal with.

This was the way the queen was able to escape and save herself. On top of this, the harm she had done was the reason why she won a greater reputation with Xerxes. For it is reported that the king, watching the battle, saw her charge the ship, and one of the men standing with him said, "O King, do you see how well Artemisia fights and how she has sunk an enemy ship?" Xerxes asked whether it were really Artemisia who had done this and they said that she had, for they were sure of the flag that was flying on her ship; and so they believed that the ship she had destroyed belonged to the enemy. Everything, as I said, turned out to be lucky for Artemisia, and one piece of luck was that no one from the ship of Calydna survived to be her accuser. The report is that when Xerxes heard what was told him, he said, "My men have become women, and my women men."

There was hard fighting; and Xerxes' brother, the admiral Ariabignes, was killed. Numbers of Persians and their allies were lost, for they did not know how to swim, and when their ships sank they were drowned; but the Greeks whose ships were sunk or who were thrown into the sea in the fighting swam to Salamis, for all the Greeks could swim.

Most of the Persian vessels were lost when their ships in the front rank were beaten, and turned to flee, for the commanders of the ships in the rear continued to press forward in order to show their bravery before the king. So the ships coming forward and the ships retreating got in each other's way.

A ship of the island of Samothrace, which had been compelled to join Xerxes' fleet, charged and rammed an Athenian ship; but while the Athenian vessel was going down, a ship of Aegina rammed the Samothracian ship and sank it. The Samothracians used the javelin as their chief weapon, and before their own ship sank they had time to discharge a shower of javelins which swept the fighting men off the ship that had just rammed theirs, and so they were able to board that ship and capture it for themselves.

Xerxes watched the fighting from his throne on the slope of a hill on the mainland opposite Salamis, and whenever he saw any notable action of his own commanders in the battle, he asked the name of the man who had done it, and his secretaries wrote down the name of the captain and the name of his city.

When the whole force of the foreigners had been put to flight, they tried to sail back to their base at Phalerum. But the ships of Aegina waited for them in the passage between the island and the mainland through which they had to pass to reach Phalerum. The Athenians in the main part of the fighting were doing great destruction both among the foreign ships that were resisting and those that were in flight; the ones that escaped the Athenians had to follow a course that brought them into the hands of the ships from Aegina. The foreign ships that did manage to escape finally reached Phalerum, where they had the protection of the land army.

The fighters who won the greatest fame in the battle were the men of Aegina and, after them, the Athenians. One of the Athenians whose work was especially distinguished was Aminias, the captain who had pursued Artemisia. If he had know that Artemisia was in that ship, he would never have stopped before he either captured her or lost his own ship. This was the order that had been given to the Athenian commanders, and there was a reward of ten thousand drachmas for the person who captured her alive, for the Athenians were very angry that a woman should have come to attack Athens. But Artemisia, as I have said, escaped.

While the sea fighting was going on, Aristides, whose outstanding qualities I have mentioned, took a number of the Athenian heavy-armed soldiers who had been stationed on the shore of Salamis and transported them to the island of Psyttalea, where they slew all the Persians that were on the little island.

When the battle at sea was broken off, the Greeks collected all the disabled ships and wrecks that were still afloat at the scene of the battle and towed them to Salamis; and having cleared the water, they kept themselves ready for another naval battle, expecting that the king would make another effort, using the ships that were left to him. But a west wind caught many of the wrecks and drove them on to the shore of Attica.

THE PERSIANS RETREAT

Xerxes finally realized the extent of his loss, and he began to be afraid that the Greeks would sail to the Hellespont and break up the bridges so that he would be cut off in Europe and run the risk of being destroyed. He dispatched the fleet to the Hellespont and set out with the army to march back to Asia.

The king had already sent a message to Susa to announce the burning of Athens, but now he had to send a second message with the news of his defeat at Salamis. There is no human power that moves more swiftly than these royal messengers. The report is that there are men and horses stationed along the royal road that leads from Asia to the capital, corresponding to the number of days required for the whole journey. The distance from Sardis to Susa is covered in thirty days of continuous riding, and for a messenger to reach Sardis from the coast of Asia opposite Greece required another three days. At regular intervals a horse and a man are ready, prepared to make a day's journey; and neither snow nor rain nor heat nor darkness keep them from completing their appointed course at top speed. The first rider hands on his dispatches to the second, the second to the third, and so the message goes from hand to hand, just like the torch races among the Greeks.

The Persians marched through Thrace and crossed the Hellespont in their ships, for they found that the bridges were no longer in order but had been broken by the storm. When they had made the crossing, they stopped to rest, and they were given more food to eat than they had on the march into Greece. They filled themselves without any discipline, and as a result of this and of the change of drinking water, many died. Xerxes and the rest went on to Sardis.

THE GREEKS
DIVIDE
THE SPOIL

The Greeks had set out in pursuit of the Persian fleet but had not been able to catch up with it. They returned to Salamis and first set apart for the gods, as was customary, the first fruits of what they had captured. Chiefly these were three Phoenician warships, one of which was dedicated to the gods at the Isthmus —where it was until my own time—another at Sunium, the cape at the eastern tip of Attica, and the third, dedicated to Ajax, at Salamis.

Then they divided the spoil among themselves and sent the first fruits as an offering to Delphi. From these the statue of a man was made, eighteen feet high, holding in his hand the prow of a ship. This stood with the gold statue of Alexander of Macedon.

When they had divided up the spoil, the Greeks sailed to the Isthmus to give the prize for excellence to that man among all the Greeks who had proved himself the most worthy of it in the war. The commanders met at the altar of Poseidon to cast their votes for first and second place. Since each thought he had been first in the fighting, he voted for himself on first place; but most of them agreed in giving second place to Themistocles. So all the other commanders had one vote each but Themistocles was far ahead of anyone else in the votes for second place. The Greeks were all too jealous to come to a decision; each commander sailed away to his own city and no award was made. But Themistocles was the man everybody talked about and he was celebrated in all Greece as by far the wisest man of the Greeks.

Appendix

PEOPLE, PLACES AND DEITIES
MENTIONED IN THE BOOK

PLACES

Abae, town in Phocis at which there was an oracle.

Abydos, a Greek city on the Asiatic side of the Hellespont.

Aegean Sea, the sea between Greece and Asia Minor.

Aegina, a large island south of Salamis.

Aeglea, an island between Eretria and Marathon.

Aphidnae, an ancient town of Attica.

Arcadia, a mountainous region in the central Peloponnesus under the domination of Sparta.

Areopagus, the "Hill of Ares" in Athens, northwest of the Acropolis.

Argos, a city in the Argive plain.

Artemisium, a cape on the northeast coast of Euboea.

Assia, the region around Susa.

Athens, capital of Attica, named for its protector, the goddess Athena.

Athos, a promontory extending from the southern coast of Macedonia.

Attica, the easternmost region of central Greece, and the territory of Athens.

Babylon, one of the great cities of the ancient world and the winter residence of the Persian king.

Boeotia, a region in central Greece, bordering on Attica.

Branchidae (also called Didyma), near Miletus, seat of an oracle of Apollo.

Calydna, a Greek city on the southwest coast of Asia Minor.

Cappadocia, the central region of Asia Minor, west of the Euphrates and north of Cilicia.

Carystos, town in Euboea, conquered by the Persians in 490 B.C.

Caspian Sea, the inland sea east of the Euxine Sea, forming the northern boundary of Persia.

Chersonese, the modern Gallipoli peninsula, extending into the Aegean along the European side of the Hellespont.

Cilicia, a region along the southern coast of Asia Minor.

Clazomenae, city on the west coast of Asia Minor, on the Gulf of Smyrna.

Corinth, city on the isthmus between northern and southern Greece, in control of communications by land and by sea.

Cynosarges, suburb east of Athens containing a sanctuary of Herakles and a gymnasium.

Delos, an island in the Aegean, legendary birthplace of Apollo and Artemis, with a famous sanctuary.

Delphi, on the slopes of Mount Parnassus, an ancient and most sacred sanctuary in Greece.

Dodona, in Epirus, seat of an ancient and important oracle of Zeus.

Eleusis, the most important town of Attica after Athens and Piraeus.

Ephesus, city on the west coast of Asia Minor, captured by Croesus.

Eretria, city in Euboea, burned by the expedition of Darius.

Euboea, the largest island in the Aegean Sea, lying along the coasts of Attica, Boeotia, and Thessaly.

Euphrates River, the western river of Mesopotamia, on which Babylon was built.

Euxine Sea, the modern Black Sea; the Greek name Euxine means "Friendly to Strangers."

Halicarnassus, a city on the southern part of the west coast of Asia Minor; birthplace of Herodotus.

Halys River, "the Salt River," in Asia Minor; flows into the Euxine Sea.

Hellespont, the narrow strait connecting the Sea of Marmara (called the Propontis) with the Aegean.

Hermus River, in western Asia Minor; flows into the Gulf of Smyrna.

Ionia, the west coast of Asia Minor, so named from the Ionian Greeks who settled there.

Isthmus of Corinth, the narrow neck of land joining northern and southern Greece, controlled by the city of Corinth.

Lacedaemon; *see* Sparta.

Laurium, mountain near Cape Sunium in Attica, containing a large mine producing both silver and lead.

Libya, the region along the north coast of Africa, west of Egypt.

Locris. Eastern Locris consisted of the mainland coast of the strait of Euboea, along the route from Thermopylae into Greece.

Lydia, kingdom in western Asia Minor ruled by Croesus whose capital was Sardis.

Macedonia, the region connecting the Balkan peninsula with Greece.

Magnesia, a region along the coast of Thessaly.

Malis, a small region in Greece near Thermopylae.

Mantinea, a city in Arcadia.

Marathon, a plain on the northeast Attic coast near a deep bay, where the Greeks defeated the Persians 490 B.C.

Media, land southwest of the Caspian Sea, whose people were related to the Persians. Originally independent, the Medes were finally conquered by the Persians.

Miletus, city on the west coast of Asia Minor.

Mycenae, an ancient city in the Argive plain.

Naxos, an island in the Aegean, sacked by the Persians 490 B.C.

Nisaean Plain, extensive plains in the mountain district of Media, north of Persia.

Orchomenus, a town in Arcadia. There was a town of the same name in Boeotia.

Parthenian Hills, a mountain range on the frontiers of Arcadia and Argolis, sacred to Pan.

150

Peloponnesus, "Island of Pelops," the large peninsula which forms the southern part of Greece, below the Isthmus of Corinth.

Persia. The organization of the Persian Empire, with the capital at Susa, was begun by Cyrus 559-529 B.C. and completed by Darius 521-486 B.C.

Phalerum, ancient harbor of Athens, east of Piraeus, which later became the chief harbor.

Phlius, a city in the northeastern part of the Peloponnesus.

Phocis, a region of central Greece.

Phoenicia, a region on the coast of Syria; the chief cities were Tyre, Sidon, and Aradus.

Plataea, a town in Boeotia, which joined Athens at Marathon.

Pontus, the region of northern Asia Minor, along the southern shore of the Euxine Sea.

Psyttalea, island between Salamis and the coast of Attica.

Salamis, a large island in the gulf off the west coast of Attica.

Salamis, the chief city of Cyprus, on the east coast.

Samos, an island off the west coast of Asia Minor, which furnished ships for the fleet of Xerxes.

Samothrace, an island in the northeastern part of the Aegean Sea.

Sardis, capital of Lydia.

Sciathus, an island north of Euboea and east of the Magnesian coast of Thessaly.

Scythia, the region between the Carpathian mountains and the river Don.

Sidon, city on the coast of Phoenicia.

Sinope, a town on the southern shore of the Euxine Sea.

Siris, a Greek colony in southern Italy.

Sparta, region in the Peloponnese, also called Lacedaemon.

Strymon River, formed the eastern boundary of Macedonia.

Sunium, promontory at the southern tip of Attica.

Susa, capital of Darius and the chief treasury of the Persian Empire.

Tegea, a town in the Arcadian plain on the road to Sparta.

Tenos, an island near Delos; its people were compelled to serve in the fleet of Xerxes.

Thebes, city in Boeotia; supported the Persians in 480-479 B.C.

Thermopylae ("Hot Gates"), a narrow passage, connecting Thessaly and Phocis, forming the only convenient route from the northern part of Greece to Attica. The coast line has changed since ancient times so that the ground no longer shows what the

pass was like at the time of the defense by the
Greeks.

Thespiae, the chief town in southern Boeotia.

Thessaly, a region in northern Greece.

Thrace, the part of the Balkan peninsula east of Macedonia, under the control of Persia, 512-479 B.C.

Tyre, a city on the Phoenician coast, south of Sidon.

PEOPLE
AND
DEITIES

Ajax, Greek hero. A captured Persian ship was dedicated to him at Salamis.

Aeschines, son of Nothon, one of the leading men of
Eretria.

Alcimachus; *see* Euphorbus.

Alcmaeon, mythological hero, son of Amphiaraus.

Alcmeonidae, a noble family in Athens.

Alexander, king of Macedon, *ca.* 495-450 B.C. (not the
same as Alexander the Great of Macedon). There
was a gold statue of him at Delphi.

Aminias, distinguished commander of an Athenian ship at Salamis.

Amphiaraus, mythological hero for whom a famous oracular shrine was named.

Apollo, one of the gods worshipped by all the Greeks. His oracle at Delphi was one of the chief Greek shrines.

Ares, god of war. The Areopagus at Athens was the "Hill of Ares."

Ariabignes, brother of Xerxes, Persian admiral at Salamis.

Aristides, *ca.* 520-468 B.C., Athenian statesman, known as "the Honest Man."

Aristogiton; *see* Harmodius.

Artabanus, uncle of Xerxes, accompanied him on the invasion of Greece.

Artaphernes, nephew of Darius, one of the commanders in the invasion of Greece.

Artemis, goddess of the moon, daughter of Zeus, sister of Apollo.

Artemisia, queen of Halicarnassus, accompanied Xerxes' expedition.

Artobazanes, son of Darius.

Artoxerxes, son of Xerxes, king of Persia, 464-424 B.C.

Astyages, king of the Medians, father of Cyrus' mother.

Athena, patron goddess of Athens.

Atossa, queen of Darius.

Biton; *see* Cleobis.

Callimachus, Athenian commander-in-chief at Marathon.

Cineas; *see* Philagrus.

Cissians, a people who were tributaries of Persia, living at the head of the Persian Gulf.

Cleobis and Biton, two Argive brothers, whose mother was a priestess of Hera. Their statues at Delphi have been discovered.

Cleomenes, king of Sparta, *ca.* 519-487 B.C., older half-brother of Leonidas.

Croesus, last king of Lydia, *ca.* 560-546 B.C.

Cynegirus, son of Euphorion, heroic Athenian killed at Marathon.

Cyrus, founder of the Persian Empire, 559-529 B.C.

Darius, king of Persia, 521-486 B.C.

Datis, a Median, general of Darius.

Demaratus, Spartan king, *ca.* 510-491 B.C., who accompanied Xerxes to Greece in 480 B.C.

Dieneces, one of the Spartan heroes at Thermopylae.

Epialtes of Malis, traitor at Thermopylae.

Euphorbus, son of Alcimachus, traitor in Eretria.

Euphorion; *see* Cynegirus.

Eurybiades, Spartan admiral, in command at battle of Artemisium.

Gaumata, usurper of the Persian throne before the reign of Darius.

Harmodius and Aristogiton, patriotic Athenians who murdered Hipparchus (514 B.C.).

Hera, goddess, wife of Zeus. Her most ancient place of worship was Argos.

Herakles, the most popular of Greek heroes, famous for his fabulous Labors.

Hipparchus, younger son of Pisistratus. Associated with his older brother Hippias. *See* Harmodius.

Hippias, tyrant of Athens, 527-510 B.C., son and successor of Pisistratus.

Hydarnes, Persian general, who led "The Immortals" at Marathon.

Hyroeades, a soldier in the Persian army at the capture of Sardis.

Hystaspes, governor of a province in Persia, father of Darius.

Leonidas ("Little Lion"), *ca.* 487-480 B.C., king of Sparta, commander of the Greeks at Thermopylae.

Leontiades, general of the Thebans at Thermopylae.

Mardi, a nomad tribe serving with Cyrus at the siege of Sardis.

Mardonius, Persian general, relative of Darius, who planned Darius' invasion of Greece.

Megebazus, a general of Darius.

Megistias, seer at Thermoypylae.

Miltiades, *ca.* 550-489 B.C., Athenian general, won the battle of Marathon.

Nothon; *see* Aeschines.

Pallas, title of the goddess Athena.

Pan, Arcadian god, with a body partly of a man, partly of a goat.

Phidippides, a long distance runner, who carried the news of the Persians to Sparta.

Philagrus, son of Cineas, traitor in Eretria.

Pisistratus, tyrant of Athens, 560-527 B.C.

Poseidon, god of the sea and of earthquakes.

Pythia, title given to the priestess who pronounced oracles in the temple of Apollo at Delphi.

Sacae, name applied by the Persians to the Scythians.

Sicinnus, slave of Themistocles, carried a message to the Persian admirals before Salamis.

Solon, *ca.* 640-560 B.C., Athenian statesman and poet.

Stesilaus, son of Thrasylaus, Athenian general killed at Marathon.

Tellus, an Athenian who died a noble death in battle.

Thales of Miletus, early sixth century B.C., one of the Seven Sages, statesman and scientist.

Themistocles, *ca.* 528-*ca.* 462 B.C., Athenian statesman.

Thrasylaus; *see* Stesilaus.

Trophonius, a Boeotian god who responded to worship-
pers through oracles at his shrine at Lebadea.

Xerxes, son of Darius, king of Persia, 485-465 B.C.

Zeus, the principal Greek God, "Father of gods and
men" in Homer.

GLANVILLE DOWNEY

Glanville Downey was born in Baltimore, Maryland. He received both his bachelor's and doctoral degrees from Princeton. A member of an archaeological expedition to Antioch, Syria, he also spent two years in Athens with the American School of Classical Studies. From 1945 to 1964 he was associated with the Dumbarton Oaks Research Library and Collection of Harvard in Washington, becoming a professor in 1960. He has written a number of books, including *Belisarius: Young General of Byzantium*. Dr. Downey is currently a professor of history and classics at Indiana University.

ENRICO ARNO

Enrico Arno was born in Germany and studied painting in Berlin. In 1947 he came to the United States and now lives in Sea Cliff, Long Island. His work varies in size from a postage stamp to a seventeen-foot mural for an office building, and in scope from teaching lettering and design to illustrations for books, record covers, and magazines.